Advance Praise for Common Ground, Uncommon Gifts . . .

Reading at times like a thriller, *Common Ground, Uncommon Gifts* is no ordinary self-help book. Rather, it is a manual for self-discovery in the deepest sense. By sharing her personal experiences traveling the Medicine Wheel, Barbara Meyers gives us tools to mine the depths of our soul in our natural environment. If we take it to heart, it may well be the best outline available for leading us into the next transformative stage on the planet.

Winter Robinson, M.Ed., author of *Intuitions, Seeing With the Heart,* and *A Hidden Order.*

In her book, *Common Ground, Uncommon Gifts,* Barbara Meyers weaves her personal stories, sharing perspective and asking questions useful to any age group as they walk their path around the Wisdom Wheel of life. Her reflections and practices encourage others to uncover their own magnificent possibilities which are just waiting to be made manifest. Barbara embraces both nature and soul as guides accessible to us all, while offering us a way to simplify and find our common ground, in what we often tend to make a complex world.

Sandra Corcoran, M.Ed. author of *Between the Dark and the Daylight Awakening to Shamanism*

This book is a triumph! It is a delicious journey through experience, not laboured/belaboured concepts, but succulent, redolent, and resonant experience. Barbara Meyers has opened the double doors of her consciousness and her heart and invited us into the journey of her life told in teaching tales. In following the stories she has lived, we meet our own blind alleys, opportunities seized, paths not followed, and breathtaking breakthroughs. *Common Ground, Uncommon Gifts* brings us a vision of a life actively lived, a life that is what a life should be: a labyrinth in which to explore, risk, and ultimately share with others the discoveries of being alive. It is said that life is what happens while you are making other plans. Life is also what happens when you open your eyes and ears and tongue and nose and touch and soul, and notice, in present or past, what you have just learned. May we not die without noticing that we have been here! Barbara teaches us to notice, with depth and grace, the many levels at which we are here in any moment, and to weave it back into the evolving fabric of all existence of which we are an essential part. She teaches us that we cannot plan life, but we can meet it. This book is an elder's blessing from one of the youngest hearts I know. Let it bless you.

Tracey Alysson, Ph. D., author of
Dying and Living In the Arms of Love:
One Woman's Journey Around Mount Kailash.

COMMON GROUND, UNCOMMON GIFTS

*Growing Peace and Harmony
through Stories, Reflections, and Practices
in the Natural World*

Barbara A. Meyers, MSW

BALBOA.
PRESS
A DIVISION OF HAY HOUSE

Interior Graphics/Art Credit: Meghan Lewis

Balboa Press books may be ordered through booksellers or by contacting:

Balboa Press
A Division of Hay House
1663 Liberty Drive
Bloomington, IN 47403
www.balboapress.com
1-(877) 407-4847

ISBN: 978-1-4525-5170-8 (sc)
ISBN: 978-1-4525-5173-9 (e)

Library of Congress Control Number: 2012908044

Because of the dynamic nature of the Internet, any web addresses or links contained in this book may have changed since publication and may no longer be valid. The views expressed in this work are solely those of the author and do not necessarily reflect the views of the publisher, and the publisher hereby disclaims any responsibility for them.

The author of this book does not dispense medical advice or prescribe the use of any technique as a form of treatment for physical, emotional, or medical problems without the advice of a physician, either directly or indirectly. The intent of the author is only to offer information of a general nature to help you in your quest for emotional and spiritual well-being. In the event you use any of the information in this book for yourself, which is your constitutional right, the author and the publisher assume no responsibility for your actions.

Any people depicted in stock imagery provided by Thinkstock are models, and such images are being used for illustrative purposes only.
Certain stock imagery © Thinkstock.

Printed in the United States of America

Balboa Press rev. date: 06/26/2012

Dedication

To all the ancestors who have gone before,
to all my elders, whose wisdom, regardless of age,
has brought light to my journey,
and to all those who will come after and continue
to light the way.

Prologue

May the lessons of the Earth Mother touch me,
May the memories of the guardians dance with me,
May the truths of the circle speak to me,
So that I may voice the gifts of the
life-force beyond time.

Acknowledgements

Daily I am touched by those with whom I share this planet. This book has a single author in title only. What lives between the book's covers are my ideas, experiences, and intentions wrapped by the influences of those who have graciously walked with me on my journey. Their love, lessons, and spirit have touched me in ways that have allowed me to bear myself and to risk being seen in the world.

Steven Foster and Meredith Little, the founders of the School of Lost Borders, first shepherded me through a formal introduction to wilderness rites of passage. Though I had already spent years exploring the natural world, it was their seminal work that opened new pathways for deepening my own transformation and provided a new paradigm for mapping human growth and development. Along with teaching staff members Joseph LaZenka, Emerald North, and Betsy Perluss, their collective ability to hold the natural and human worlds as one and to offer challenging opportunities for meeting oneself provided fertile ground for growing my own being. Thus they modeled for me ways to provide fertile ground for those whom I touch. And the circle continues . . . .

Winter Robinson, medical intuitive, clairvoyant and teacher, always works at the growing edge of creative and holistic ways to tap into the many modes of learning and knowing available to us in the world. Together with her husband, Michael, they continually challenge their own way of being in the world while challenging their friends, colleagues, and students. Their style of leading by example while allowing others to find their own solutions to living in this complex world is both refreshing and welcome as I discover ways to appropriate life for myself. It is a model that informs my work with others. And the circle continues . . . .

Sandra Corcoran, shamanic counselor, writer, teacher, and founder of Starwalker Visions, has been a guide in these last years. With a rich training in the shamanic ways of indigenous cultures throughout the Americas including the Seneca traditions, she has introduced me to new ways for gaining and using knowledge while bringing both encouragement and affirmation to my own experiences and knowing. New ways of divining truth that align with the ancestors and my own internal knowing allows me to share those gifts with others. And the circle continues . . . .

Tracey Alysson, teacher, therapist, colleague, and friend, in courageously sharing her own journey of walking the path to wholeness, has provided a beacon of light and a steady compass for my own journey. In the relentless search, the willingness to meet both the darkness and the light and the growing trust in being received without judgment, we can risk revealing the self to oneself and to another. In turn I can offer fertile ground for others to do likewise. And the circle continues . . . .

As a single homeowner and businesswoman, I soon learned that writing at home became a practical impossibility. Thus without gracious friends who offered their homes as writing getaways, this book would still be a dream. A grateful thank you goes to Mary and John Graham who offered their new home for a writing vacation; Winter and Michael Robinson, who in the guise of house- and pet-sitting, offered a peaceful woodland home on a waterfront in which to write; and Doris Birmingham, dear friend and inveterate traveler, who repeatedly made her comfortable home available to me when she was away. Lastly I wish to thank the Benedictine Monks of the Glastonbury Abbey in Hingham, Massachusetts, whose rooms and library provided a serene and spiritual setting for reading, thinking, and writing. A blend of spiritual quiet and spirited conversation over hearty meals fed both body and soul. May I offer the same to others. And the circle continues . . . .

In my lifetime, my path has intersected with those of many others—teachers, peers, students, clients, friends, and family. Each meeting has brought its challenges and its gifts. Those who are students of life are the most memorable for they have reminded me to meet life fully and to question relentlessly so as to grow into the community of all beings. Special appreciation is extended to Betsy and Jay, Olga and Jack, Cathy and

Debra, Gretchen, Cindy, Karen, and my siblings Patricia and Tom and their families for sharing their gifts of friendship and for embracing life. It is in community that we learn to give and receive. And the circle continues . . . .

I am technically challenged! Without the technical assistance of others, it would not have been possible for you to have this book in hand. With the use of computer graphics and a good deal of know-how, Meghan Lewis transformed my ideas about the Medicine Wheel and the Four Shields into the illustrations that appear herein. Fran Vainas worked magic on her computer to put my manuscript into publishable form. But her contributions go far beyond. A patient teacher, she answered my endless questions, repeated instructions more than once, walked me through which keys to press when and generously shared her knowledge of publishing. Thus with their assistance, the circle continues . . . .

Lastly, I owe a debt of gratitude to the natural world and those ancestors who learned to live in full community with their environment. Their DNA lives in us all. And I owe a similar debt to those ancestors who had the foresight, courage, and energy to act to protect, preserve, and honor the natural world. It is a wild and pristine world through which I have been shepherded safely. Now it is a world I want others to know. And the circle continues . . . .

Barbara Meyers
Bradford, NH
February 2012

Table of Contents

Preface

This book is an elder's gift to those who follow. It is written for those men and women across the life span, from young adult to elder, who are committed to living with conscious intention, curiosity, and courage while seeking to build a more equitable, generous, and compassionate world. I see them as grassroots leaders for the turning from the greed, hatred, and delusions of an industrial society to one that sustains life. Some are professionals—teachers, business men and women, civic leaders, entrepreneurs, community organizers, healthcare workers, therapists, and environmentalists among them. Many are moms and dads strongly committed to family. Others live on the edges, the result of social and economic injustice. What distinguishes all is their quest to live lives of meaning, dignity, and compassion. Courageously, they seek to move away from consumption to follow a new path. They do not have all the answers but they are willing, both individually and collectively, to address how we might meet the ever-increasing threat to the planet's climate and its impact on all life on this planet.

Over the span of my life, the natural world has been both my teacher and wisdom keeper. Not only did I seek the companionship of other sentient beings in nature, I also sought its stunning beauty and serenity. But I also went into the natural world to prove myself, to escape the judgments and manipulations of the human world, and to hide. Thus for many years I straddled these two worlds—surviving through quiet competence in the human world and being with boldness and adventure in the natural world. Always introspective, I was slowly trying to put the pieces of my life together. It was not until I was introduced to a modern application of the Native American Medicine Wheel and its four seasons and four directions that I could begin to construct a bridge connecting the self in the natural world with the self of the human world. This is a journey that continues.

The writing of this book has been a long and challenging process. Having lived a stealth-like existence in the human world, writing has brought me face-to-face with my fears of being known and seen. That has required moving beyond the vulnerability of shame and humiliation to being able to hold my full being with love and gratitude. In sharing these personal teaching stories, reflecting about meaning, and creating practices for you, the reader, I have deepened my understanding of my many trips around the Medicine Wheel and glimpse the way ahead. I invite you, the reader, to do the same.

This is a book to engage with slowly. It is meant to be savored and revisited, not to be read through cover to cover and then added to a shelf of accomplishments. Like the passage of the seasons, it can be turned to repeatedly, either alone or in the company of others— children, families, friends, communities. Its design allows it to be carried with you and referred to when out in the natural world. Our life's experiences invite us to travel ever around the Medicine Wheel so that we may grow into wise, compassionate beings ready to be stewards of all that is here. As you consult this guide throughout life's journeys, may you grow in your curiosity, creativity, compassion, and gratitude for all you will meet in yourself and others in this fragile world.

Barbara Meyers
Bradford, New Hampshire
February 2012

CHAPTER ONE

Converging Paths

All the life rhythms of the
insects—birds—flowers—animals and human beings
Concur to celebrate one great symphony . . . .
A symphony man cannot direct . . .
and should not try.
Born with great powers . . . .
Equalized by powerlessness
Man cannot beat his separate drums . . . .
Nor go his way unheeding.
For he is an inseparable part of the Universe—
Its grasses and trees—
The wind and the wings.

Gwen Frostic in The Enduring Cosmos

Furthermore, we have not even to risk the adventure
alone, for the heroes of all time have gone before
us. The labyrinth is entirely known. We have only to
follow the thread of the hero path, and where we had
thought to find an abomination, we shall find a god.
And where we had thought to slay another, we shall

ourselves. Where we had thought to travel outward, we will come to the center of our own existence. And where we had thought to be alone, we will be with all the world.

Joseph Campbell in *The Power of Myth*

A small blue moth struggles to free itself from a spider's web. Taking pity, I retrieve a small twig and free the moth. The web is ruined and, though free of the web, the moth remains trapped by the strong, silken fibers of the web. It will die a slow death unless some creature comes along to end its life. I turn and walk away. Are there things here for me to learn about myself, about community, about the hunter and the hunted, and about the circle of life?

In *Common Ground, Uncommon Gifts: Growing Peace and Harmony through Stories, Reflections, and Practices in the Natural World*, readers are led on inward journeys of discovery through outward journeys into the natural world. As such, it is a guide for individuals, families, and communities wishing to be effective stewards of their own lives and the life of the planet.

The title reflects the weaving of two concepts.

First, *Common Ground* acknowledges and celebrates that this is our planet. What is here is all there is. Every single being, whether animal, vegetable, mineral, or other substance, has a soul and shares this planet. Though many have known this through the infinity of time and space, more recently, we have lost sight of that deep knowing. With technology, industrialization, and a sense of superiority, we created dualities—man versus nature, mind versus body, sacred versus profane, us versus them, haves versus have nots, and civilized versus primitive among them. Relying on rationality and thought, we separated ourselves from the rest of life on the planet and claimed our superiority over all. Nature became a force to battle against and subdue. We demonized nature. We also demonized those who knew how to live in and with the natural world. The cost has been profound. Now we are faced with peak oil, burgeoning populations, climate change, and dwindling resources, all of which raise questions of sustainability. The cost has also been our isolation from our knowing of connection and interdependence that lives deep within our DNA.

Our deep knowing was reawakened back in 1968 when Apollo gave us the first view of planet Earth from space. The long-range view of "Earth-rise," this blue-green gem surrounded by the blackness of space, reminded us that we are all here as one. To survive and to sustain life here, we must honor the interdependence of all the beings that exist here.

That view from space helped us to re-member the words of Chief Seattle:

This we know. The earth does not belong to man; man belongs to the earth. This we know. All things are connected like the blood that unites one family. All things are connected. Whatever befalls the earth, befalls the sons of the earth. Man does not weave the web of life, he is merely a strand in it. Whatever he does to the web, he does to himself.[1]

---

[1] Joanna Macy and Molly Young Brown. *Coming Back to Life: Practices to Reconnect Our Lives, Our World* (Gabriola

Though we know this, when it comes to living what we know, we are woefully lacking. We live in a world of profiteering and consumerism. More is better—more money, more toys, more car, more house. Until I stopped watching television, I had no idea of the battering I was receiving with constant advertisements for some item I should have. Our choices are based not on need but on want. And our consumerism is the principle lever for building and sustaining our economy as well as our part of the world economy. With empty lives, how easily we fall prey to the hawking of wares. And most of this manufacturing—production, transportation, and delivery—has occurred without regard for natural resources, raw materials or the pollution of our Earth— oceans, air, and land. Now we are confronted with global warming, peak oil, water resources polluted by run-off, toxic landfills, and nuclear waste.

We have been willing participants and willing bystanders in this process. We have bought into unfettered consumerism believing it will fill our psychic emptiness. Instead we have found our emptiness unmet, while thinking that surely there is some other item that will fill us once and for all. Collectively, we have missed the mark. *I want* does not fill us. *I want* disconnects us from families, communities, states, nations, and the world. We have lost our connectedness to one another. Other beings, both human and non-human, have become mere commodities.

Island B.C., Canada: New Society Publishers, 1998), pp 197-201.

There was a time when the deep knowing of interconnectedness was honored. This was a time when human beings we often think of as primitive lived in concert with the natural world; a time when the natural world was teacher; and a time when human beings did not put themselves in the center of the circle. Not only that, but these indigenous people also knew that the Earth is not the center of the universe but that the sun is!

Of course, we cannot return to this way of life. We live in an ever more complex world. Technology is everywhere—in our hands, ears, cars, kitchens, living rooms, offices, stores, hospitals, schools, and so on. All of this continues to stress our natural resources, add to global warming, challenge our use of space and water, and raise issues of waste disposal. We celebrate our advances, but we have not weighed the consequences of these advances on our collective environment, both human and other. We have been unwilling to make hard moral and ethical choices about the costs of technology, not only to others, but also to our deeper being. Continuing on this path, not only will we bring continued destruction to this blue-green gem in the solar system, but also, in the process, we will destroy ourselves. What will we do when we cannot afford the cost of fuel to heat our homes or to run our cars and trucks? What will we do when we cannot afford the cost of food transported great distances? What will we do when there is insufficient clean water? What will we do when there is drought or the population outgrows the water source?

We are latecomers to this planet. Without any guidance or input from us humans, this planet evolved over millions of years into delicately balanced and interdependent ecosystems. When natural calamities and devastation occurred, the natural world adjusted and systems were slowly brought into a new balance. The planet's processes are primarily ones of creation and adaptation. We interlopers continue to upset nature's innate seeking of balance. The speed and degree to which we have intruded upon this delicate balance means that nature alone cannot right the wrongs. It is for us to take responsibility for our actions and seek ways to establish balance in the natural world and between the natural world and humankind.

It remains unclear what we can salvage and how we and the Earth will survive. Surely species have been lost, never to inhabit this Earth again. Global warming continues, Earth temperatures will rise, as will the water levels. We are beyond peak oil. Cataclysms occur with greater frequency. Population grows, as does the demand for food. And many questions remain. Why are there so many cancers? What do we do with nuclear waste? Why is there bee colony collapse? Why do dolphins beach themselves? Why are there so many natural disasters?

To address these problems and questions will require something more than technology. We need to be asking ourselves, "How can we re-discover what we have temporarily forgotten though it still lives within our DNA?" What must we do to re-member our *Common Ground* and re-find our rightful place in the Web of Life? The time is short.

This brings us to the second concept, *Uncommon Gifts*. The gifts are from the natural world given to us by way of our ancestors, the indigenous people who learned from their environment—the seasons, the stars, the moon and sun, the waters, and the flora and fauna. As keen observers, they learned how to survive and thrive; how to hunt, harvest, and share; how to prepare for seasonal changes by storing or migrating; how to conserve resources; and how to stay warm or to cool down. They learned how to make and use tools; how to carry, and eventually, make fire; and how to make a wheel. But their keen observations led to deeper learnings as well. These indigenous people saw their own lives reflected in the seasons—spring, summer, fall, winter and the rebirth of yet a new spring—and developed a spiritual belief system based on this knowing. They observed how groups of a single species form and live together and, from this, they developed roles for tribal members honoring the contribution of each to tribal well-being. They witnessed how important it was for the young to be transitioned into more mature roles and developed rites of passage, especially from adolescence into adulthood, to help ensure the regeneration of their society. And they saw how the old ones were honored and protected.

Their gifts to us are wisdom and humility. They learned that human beings are not the center of the Web of Life. Through experience, they learned that to disturb one strand of the web disturbs the entire web. This knowing lives in our DNA and we must find our way back to this wisdom and humility. We must learn from the wisdom keepers. To hold sacred the entire Web of Life, we must develop the moral courage to weigh the consequences of unfettered competition and consumption and the humility to take us out of the center of the web. To do that, we must also be willing to consider how we will build a regenerative human world in which our leaders in government, business, education, and religion have transitioned into healthy adulthood rather than the self-centeredness of adolescence. And we must be willing to look within ourselves and be willing to meet our own demons to grow into daring and caring adults and elders. In meeting the interior world of one's psyche, we each can come to know who we are, who we wish to become, the meaning of our life, the gifts to our community, and our place on the long strand of those who came before us and those who will follow.

When I speak of *Uncommon Gifts*, I do so not because they are rare but because we have turned our backs on what our ancestors knew. Our grandiosity and ego have taken us down the path of destruction. Now is the time to re-discover what we have chosen to forget. To return to our rightful place in the web, we can look to the natural world to help us to re-member about birth, suffering, the will to live, community, love, death, transformation, and inter-dependence.

As our ancestors knew, we have much to learn about ourselves by entering into a relationship with the natural world. *Common Ground, Uncommon Gifts* is a guide for those who wish to grow more fully into successive stages of life and wish to be an example and a force for living in concert with all that is here. This is not a book for those who wish to return to nature to live a nativist life. This is a book for mainstream people who want to live in, contribute to, and impact the world. It is a grassroots book for seekers and doers who are committed to growing peace and harmony within the self, with other human beings, and with all here on this planet. Lone individuals can use this guide for their own growth. However, I have come to understand that it is in circles of communion that we can most effectively grow, change, and influence direction. In coming together in families or small groups, we can experience the natural world, reflect, discuss, make meaning, and take action, thus setting free the seeds of change to take root in ever-expanding circles.

Common Ground, Uncommon Gifts offers opportunities for individuals and communities to turn to the natural world as teacher and guide. Anecdotal stories, reflections, and practices offer opportunities for looking deeply into one's own journey. In developing ways to live mindfully in the world and to find *common ground* with all that is here, one is free to bring one's gifts more fully into the world of all beings, human and other.

I have chosen stories for two reasons. First, as an elder woman, I look back on my experiences in the natural world with both humility and gratitude for the teachings. I have been knocked down by the forces of nature, I have confronted many fears, and I have been lifted up in joy and wonder. These experiences have helped me to become more fully human. How can I not share these teachings, for I know these are not uncommon experiences for those who seek meaning and purpose in life.

Despite the considerable interest in self-growth and in finding purpose for being born into this time and place, most of us have not considered the natural world as teacher because of the duality between man and nature. Growth is a forever process and happens in a variety of milieus. What growth asks of us is a willingness to "let go," to not be bound by the known, and to be in the here and now. To do so requires both curiosity and courage. The natural world presents a ready and often unknown arena for meeting ourselves as well as other beings in this world. In so doing, we can find our *common ground*.

Second, storytelling is the oldest form of teaching. Regardless of its form or format, be it oral, visual, written, fiction, non-fiction, or poetic, story pulls the witness into adventure and experience so that the witness becomes participant. In these moments, deeper levels of consciousness both in the individual soul and in the collective are made manifest. In telling stories of the self meeting the natural world, the intent is to become a guide for those who wish to explore this "other" world as a resource for growth, meaning making, and connection. In the interface between self and nature, we find our rightful place in the Web of Life and become more effective stewards of the entire web.

Each story is followed by a reflection. Reflections are intended to take a single story and place it in the context of the larger story of one's life journey, others' journeys, and our connection to community—both human and natural. Through metaphor, hitching onto other stories, or reflecting on the here and now of everyday life, the intention is to re-discover the strands that connect us one to another and to all that is here. Reflections give us pause so that we can go deeper.

As a teacher, I am committed to experience being the consummate teacher. Whereas reading a story plants a seed in the mind that can be cultivated into action, experience demands a presence and a commitment that creates meaning and memory not only in the mind but in the fullness of one's being. We are more than mind. The practices offered herein can be done alone or with others. The intention is that they will reverberate, expand, and connect the doer more deeply with him/herself and with the larger world, both human and beyond. Many of these experiences can be done with children as written while others need to be modified and require supervision. Children are our future and carry our hopes for an Earth of balance and health. Beyond that, when we undertake these experiences with children, we discover the wonder and the spontaneity of the child-part that lives within each of us.

The stories, reflections, and practices are organized around the Native American Medicine Wheel. The Medicine Wheel holds the four cardinal directions and the four seasons of the year as well as the four seasons of a life: east, spring and birth; south, summer and childhood; west, fall and adolescence; and north, winter and adulthood. The arc of the circle between north and east holds elderhood, death and then rebirth in the east. The Medicine Wheel honors the *Common Ground* of all beings here on the Earth. It reflects the wisdom and humility of the indigenous people.

CHAPTER TWO

The Medicine Wheel

The Circle

Everything that the Power of the World does is done
in a circle.
The sky is round and I have heard that the earth is
round like a ball and so are all the stars.
The wind, in its great power, whirls.
Birds make their nests in circles for theirs is the same
religion as ours.
The sun goes forth and goes down again in a circle.
The moon does the same and both are round.
Even the seasons form a great circle in their changing
and always come back again to where they
were.
The life of man is a circle from childhood to
childhood.
And so it is in everything where power moves.

Black Elk (1863-1950)

Within the circles of our lives
we dance the circles of the years,
the circles of the seasons
within the cycles of the moon
within the circles of the seasons,
the circles of our reasons
within the cycles of the moon . . . .
The circles turn
each giving into each, into all.
Only music keeps us here.

Wendell Berry Song (4) in
Collected Poems 1957-1982

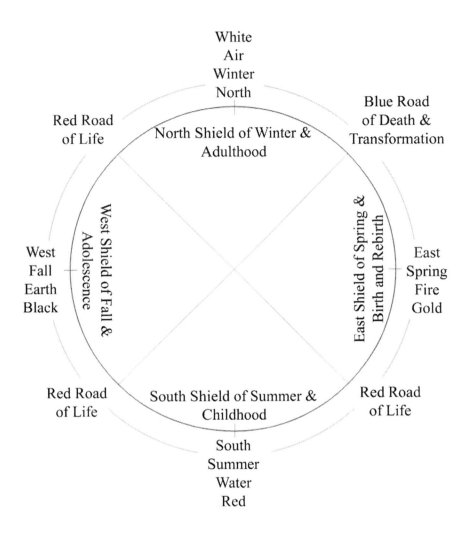

The Medicine Wheel

Concept from Steven Foster, *The Four Shields*

Illustrations by Meghan Lewis

To survive, our earliest ancestors had to live within the laws of nature. A oneness with the natural world was needed and, without that, we would not be here.

With growing consciousness of their environment, our ancestors developed a keen awareness of the natural world's cycles—the four seasons, night and day, phases of the moon, abundance and scarcity, and birth to death to rebirth. With this knowledge, they learned to harvest, store, conserve, and share. To ensure not only their own survival but the survival of the tribe, our ancestors transmitted this knowledge to succeeding generations through rituals marking the Earth's seasonal path around the sun and the passage of human life from birth through childhood, adolescence, adulthood, elderhood, and death.

For many of these emerging cultures in widely separated parts of the world, the Circle or Mandela became the template by which consciousness and knowing was taught and passed onto succeeding generations. The Circle or Mandela held all—the essence of time, a single experience, a single life, and the life force of a tribe or community. It represented coming full circle from beginning to end. The circle continues to have meaning in today's indigenous cultures and that meaning is there for us as well.

THE CIRCLE OF A DAY

In looking at the Circle as a representation of twenty-four hours, the circle begins in the east with the sunrise. Slowly the sky and the clouds turn from deep purple to pink to orange to yellow as the Earth's rotation returns the sun's light to us. At first just a glow, then the sky in the east brightens and soon a small arc of the sun emerges out of the sea or the prairie. In the mountains the sunrise is hidden in the east and is caught only by watching the mountains in the west being transformed from silhouetted monoliths to three dimensional peaks of pink, then orange, and finally yellow. Slowly the life of the night beings gives way to that of the day. As the sun's warmth penetrates the landscape, the bird chorus reaches its crescendo.

On the circle, the sun continues clockwise to the south and the heat of midday. Above ground much of the natural world takes a rest. Yet the hawks and vultures still circle lazily in the sky. The sun's heat is penetrating deep into the earth where the juices of life stir as plant life draws sustenance from both the heat and the light. Microorganisms are doing their work, too, recycling death and decay in preparation for new life.

The path on the circle continues to the west and the dying of the day when the hues of the morning sky are reversed—yellow to orange to pink to purple. The creatures of the day eat their last meal before bedding down for the night. The day's sounds are stilled and the night sounds emerge—cricket songs and tree frog choruses.

The darkness of the night brings us to the north on the circle. Owls hoot, bats swoop, and the wolves howl as they go forth to hunt their prey. On a clear night, the infinity of the universe is displayed. The constellations

circle the North Star. Cygnus the Swan flies from north
to south through the sky. The Earth continues to turn
and night gives way to the beginning of a new day in
the east.

THE CIRCLE OF THE SEASONS

In the year the Earth travels a circular path around the
sun, the four seasons are experienced by all Earth's
beings. Just as the circle marks a single day, it is
also used to mark the passage of the seasons. The
circle of seasons begins in the east with the season
of spring and birth or rebirth. Though the beginning
of each season is marked by a specific day, each
season extends over a period of time. Both before
and after the official beginning of spring, new life
is unfolding. The sap rises in the trees. Migrations
north are underway. Beneath a blanket of snow, roots
and shoots are stirring unseen. Snow buttercups and
snowdrops may push through the snow to find light.
After a long winter, we are impatient for spring. The
return of the first robin and the red wings gives us
hope which is quickly dashed by a late season snow
storm. Then almost without warning, the air warms,
the snows melt, the ice-out occurs on the last lake
and new life bursts forth from the womb of Mother
Earth and the womb of all her beings. Delicate flowers
turn their faces towards the sun's warmth. The air
is filled with the birdsong of courting. Spring rains
nurture the earth and the smells of wet soil waft

on the breeze. Delicate tree blossoms give way to tiny leaves. Spontaneously leaves break their casings and the world turns green. Everywhere there is the burgeoning of life.

Soon the earth heats up and we are on our way to the south and summer's tropical weather. This is the time of growth and maturing. Plants and leaves turn a darker hue of green and fruits begin to appear on stems and stalks. Bird parents exhaustively feed, then fledge their first brood, and may even begin a second family. The young of the four-leggeds stay close to their mothers and learn the ways of their species. Their playful exuberance is tempered by learning how to forage for food and how to stay safe from predators. The smells of the first hay harvest fill the summer air. With heat and humidity, thunder clouds reach high into the sky and fresh rains plummet to a welcoming earth. With warmth and rain, a second hay harvest becomes possible. Butterflies emerge from their cocoons. While all is left to grow and ripen, the local swimming hole becomes a place of respite.

Now we are well on our way to the west and fall, the season of harvest and preparation for winter. Fruits and vegetables are picked and stored. Grains are harvested for winter use. Birds, ducks, and geese begin to flock in preparation for their journeys southward. Seeds, borne by the wind, land in new places. Large four-leggeds mate so that new beings may gestate through the winter months. The leaves of the deciduous trees lose their chlorophyll, and the resulting reds, oranges, and yellows please happy "leaf-peepers." There is coolness and less humidity in the air. The smell of decay lurks about. The sound of the thrush is silenced. Sap withdraws into the trunk and descends into the darkness of earth-bound roots. Next spring's new leaves are tight, little buds. Though these buds hold the promise of spring, we must turn our attention to the coming winter so the garden is put to bed, the firewood is stacked, and the house is closed in. At the same time animal life is preparing. The squirrels are harvesting and storing their winter stash. All are busy finding winter housing.

Fall runs into winter as the circle moves around to the north. The deadened world of browns and grays receives its first blanket of white. Some of nature's creatures begin their winter naps. Stillness descends to be broken occasionally by the strident calls of the blue jay alerting others to an intruder. Delicate snowflakes or driven crystals continue to blanket the earth. Frigid air descends from the north. The lakes freeze. The footprints of nature's hunters dot the unbroken snow. On warmer winter days, a red squirrel may dart from its den to collect newly fallen seeds and then rush back home. Spring's growth rests beneath the insulation of winter's snows. The stream's voice is reduced to a murmur. The late winter stillness may be broken by a loud "Boom" as a crack in the lake's ice darts across the lake and echoes through the stillness. In winter, it is as if the natural world holds its collective breath waiting to be awakened by the return of the sun.

As the path continues around the circle towards spring, the sap begins to rise, the geese head north, the red wings return, the snows begin to melt during the day only to freeze up again at night, and the stream quickens. The circle is complete. Spring returns and the path around the circle begins anew.

THE CIRCLE OF LIFE

In the natural world, the circle can be a metaphor for the circle of a single life—birth followed by growth through various stages to ripening and maturing then decline to death and a return to the womb of Mother Earth to be born anew. Some of nature's beings complete this circle once in a lifetime. They are born, mature, produce seeds or eggs, die, and provide sustenance for others. The mayfly's journey is brief. Annual plants travel around the circle in a calendar year whereas perennials and trees travel around the circle many times. Many birds and mammals also travel around the circle many times as they pass through the seasons of their lives before life comes to an end.

Farmers, hunters, gatherers, and others living close to the earth know intimately the seasonal cycle of the circle, for their livelihood and survival depend on that knowing. Through living close to the rhythms of nature as well as acknowledging themselves as part of nature, they have also come to see the circle of the seasons as a metaphor for the seasons of their own lives. Viewed through this metaphor, one's life begins in the east with birth, moves clockwise through childhood in the south, to adolescence in the west, to adulthood in the north, to elderhood and finally death as we return to spring and rebirth in some form.

Many indigenous people saw the circle of the seasons as something more than a reflection of our physical life on Earth. To be viable, every society must hold regeneration of its society as the primary focus. The question was and is, "How is self-knowledge and self-consciousness developed so that a person can become part of community consciousness and thus contribute to the regeneration of the tribe or society?" This significant question focuses us not on just one life but the life of the entire community.

Indigenous societies took this question very seriously and nurtured self-knowledge and self-consciousness throughout the stages of life. Focusing on wholeness of the person, their teaching attended to not only the physical but also the mental, emotional, and spiritual development of each person. Thus a way to look at the circle and the developmental stages of childhood, adolescence, adulthood, and elderhood is to track the tasks of each stage as the person transitions to becoming a contributing member of the tribe or community. The emphasis then is not just on physical growth but also on the mental, emotional, and spiritual development of the person.

In childhood then the tasks are to grow into one's body, to learn how to control the body in space, to play, to attune to the others in the community, to allow oneself to be held emotionally by the community, to explore the tasks of adulthood through games, and to be present in the community's rituals. With the emergence of adolescence, the child must leave behind childish things and enter into the rituals of darkness to find his or her individual strengths and talents, and to undertake training in those talents. Again, though grounded in puberty and body changes, there is a simultaneous focus on mental, emotional, and spiritual growth as the young person seeks to find his or herself and moves into that tribe's or community's subgroup. In adulthood, the tasks are to lead and to share one's knowledge and skills so that the tribe or community can be sustained within the confines of the natural world. Here ego is subservient to the group. And in elderhood, one's accumulated wisdom and knowledge are shared willingly and gratefully received by the community.

THE NEW MEDICINE WHEEL[2]

The circle was and is an important symbol in many Meso-American tribes. Some turned the circle into a medicine wheel or hoop to represent all of life. The wheel or hoop symbolizes their deep knowledge of the natural world and the interdependence of all things on the planet including humans. Each of the four Cardinal points on the wheel represents one of the four directions, one of the four seasons and one of the four elements of life—air, fire, water and earth.

---

[2] Steven Foster and Meredith Little, *The Four Shields: The Initiatory Seasons of Human Nature* (Big Pine, CA: Lost Borders Press, 1998).

Steven Foster and Meredith Little, founders of the School of Lost Borders, took the Medicine Wheel teachings of their own teachers, their personal work in the wilderness, and their work as guides to others seeking self-consciousness and adapted the Medicine Wheel for today's seekers. By adding the physical, mental, emotional, and spiritual elements of the seasons of our lives to the wheel, they have provided both a map and a compass to help us live more realized lives both for ourselves and our communities. Their application of the Medicine Wheel to modern-day life can mirror for us where we are on the Wheel as we negotiate life's challenges—education, relationships, child-rearing, career, and community member among them. Each of these challenges has the potential for taking us around the Medicine Wheel many times as we consider choices and problem-solve daily. For example, just consider the multiple challenges we face as parents, caregivers, and teachers in raising children from birth through adolescence and into adulthood. And then the challenges are still not over as we find ourselves reforming our relationships with our adult children and grandchildren.

Each experience that we encounter, when taken as a totality, can be seen as completing one circuit around the Medicine Wheel, for each experience has a beginning, transitions through several stages, and an ending to that experience as well as a beginning to a yet another experience. When viewed from this perspective, one can appreciate how one experience can be used to build upon another experience. These multiple travels around the Wheel can then be viewed holographically as a spiral as one learning is stacked upon another and so on. Each experience allows us to build upon the learning from past experiences while presenting new challenges that initiate us into yet new learning and growth. This is the way of life.

East Shield

We are born in the east. The east is the place of rebirth and regeneration. Without birthing, nothing can grow, so the east is the source of all life in the broadest sense. It is the place of light, of the rising sun, of enlightenment that sources all life. What is here on the Earth is all there is, all that is born must come from what is already here. Thus birth cannot occur without the death of something, which in turn sustains new life.

As human beings, we enter the world as helpless, wailing infants. If we are held with love, joy, and nurture, the world becomes a place of curiosity and wonder. Not only do we come to know the sweet taste of mother's milk but we are comforted by the warmth and love of her touch, the sound of her voice, her laughter, the sight of her smiling face, and the relief of her presence. We are comforted, too, by all those who surround us with love and life. With such safety and support, we are launched from infancy into toddlerhood and the early stages of childhood. Everything is new—tastes, colors, sounds, touch, and feelings. Everything is adventure.

Of course, this is the ideal, but the journey for some begins not so easily. With abuse, neglect, and/ or abandonment, the journey has many pitfalls, and an infant or toddler will learn to respond to the world in a much different manner. Distrust and fear lead to wariness and withdrawal, a diminished ability to attach to caretakers, and the death of curiosity and joy. When an infant or toddler faces physical, mental, or emotional survival, the normal developmental milestones are delayed or absent. A profound emptiness slows the journey to childhood.

South Shield

With a shower of protection and love, we move into the south and childhood. This is a place of innocence, trust, and faith. We continue to explore, to be innately curious, and to play. Life is all about the self. We are in our bodies and use all five senses. Instincts and urges rule, thus the body rules the mind, soul, and spirit. We give free flow to our emotions. We laugh, cry, scream, and tantrum and are so very pleased with our accomplishments. After all, we believe the world revolves around us. "I am powerful, I am ego." But soon we come to know that the world does not just revolve around us. "Oh, there are others here!" We meet other children, grown-ups, teachers, and elders who do not always treat us as if we are the only one. With secure love and support at home, we begin to make the transition to being in community, to being one of many. Adults do give us attention but they begin to ask more of us. No longer can we just play. No longer can we have it our way. We must listen to others. We seek our place in the world and life is no longer always fun.

Those who have suffered abandonment, abuse, or neglect have a more difficult time making this transition. It is a difficult task to let go of "I" when one has lived in survival mode. If the integrity of the self was compromised early, there is a profound lack of trust and faith in others as well as in the self. The world is one of aloneness, emptiness, and anxiety and the defensive stance is to protect the self at all costs. The road to the West Shield is filled with many challenges for all but especially so for these children.

West Shield

Fall's role is to prepare the child to move into the adult world. To get there, one must move through the darkness of adolescence. Everything about me is now in flux. I am initiated into the unknown, into the darkness. What will I do? Will I try to hold onto childhood or will I look within? Will I allow my self-consciousness to lead me into introspection? Will I look into the darkness to find who I am? Will I begin to define myself as an individuated person separate from my family and others? Will I have the courage of "I am?" Will I march to my own drummer or follow others? Will I grow my self-acceptance and self-esteem? Will I begin to find my gifts to the community? These are the tasks of adolescence. It is the time of the hero's or heroine's journey. Whereas indigenous societies highly value the rites of passage of adolescence as critical to healthy emergence into adulthood, many technological societies do not mentor adolescents well, leaving them to stumble blindly to find their path. Many young people get stuck between childhood and adolescence and, though chronologically become adults, carry with them the self-centeredness of "I."

The West Shield is fraught with many challenges and fears. Teens living in loving and wise families will try their wings at independence and responsibility knowing there is a nurturing nest to which to return when they need help and support. Others, without the safety net of love and support as challenges arise, will react with anger, rage, and rebellion. Other teens are so empty and fearful that they hide in anonymity or seek others to care for them. Hiding and helplessness provide an "escape" from the pain of growing into responsible adults. Others just remain stuck.

North Shield And Beyond

If we risk growing and maturing mentally and emotionally, our hero's or heroine's journey through adolescence propels us into adulthood. Now I am free to move beyond self-love to love of others and community. With maturity I bring my gifts more fully into the world and "give away" my gifts to the community. With mindfulness I try not to fall prey to ego. I turn my rational mind, my experiences, and my wisdom into actions that enhance community, peace, and harmony.

Now with the wisdom of elderhood, I prepare for death and transformation. As my physical body deteriorates and my mental acuity diminishes, I move closer to spirit and I catch sight of my place on the long path of evolution. I have purpose and I pass my wisdom onto others with the faith and trust of new birth. And the circle continues.

Traveling Around The Medicine Wheel

We travel around the Medicine Wheel not only in a single lifetime but every day of our lives. Every experience in family, education, work, play, and social environment takes us around the Wheel. Reflect upon any experience in your life. Perhaps it was the beginning of a new job, a new activity, a marriage, a birth, a divorce, a new career, a new relationship, and so on. In the beginning you are excited, curious and a bit tentative, but you accept the challenge. This is the newness of the East Shield. You become totally focused on this new experience—learning, watching, evaluating, and being hopeful. You may even take delight in this new adventure as you move into the South Shield. There are friends, family, and mentors supporting you. At some point the "honeymoon" ends and you are tested. Suddenly you find yourself alone and having to make a decision. You are plunged into the darkness of the West

Shield. You are severed from the innocence, trust, and joy of childhood and propelled into adolescence. What do you do? Always there are choices. Do you accept the challenge? Do you run and hide? Do you cave in? Do you move into the unknown, claim your voice, grow, and continue around the Medicine Wheel into the competence and community of the North Shield? If it is the latter that occurs then you are transformed and you are ready to meet a new challenge in the east. If you remain stuck or go back to the South Shield's childhood patterns then you simply encounter another opportunity to grow and continue your path around the Wheel.

We move around the Medicine Wheel again and again. Each time we circle around the Wheel, we grow in our fullness. Each movement in growth allows for ever more growth toward self-consciousness, peace, and harmony with self and others. Successive circuits around the Wheel create an upward spiraling effect as we continually grow and meet more challenges. This is the path of life.

In looking at the Medicine Wheel in this manner, we can honor it as a container for physical, mental, emotional, and spiritual growth. No one shield is better than another. Each is as important as the next. Each serves as a marker to inform the person and community as to where he or she is with respect to this particular experience as well as one's life journey. It is only a map and a compass.

The goal is to seek balance and to move around the Wheel without being stuck in any one shield. But we are only human. Becoming stuck is unavoidable and indicates that a particular shield is overdeveloped and that the shield directly opposite is underdeveloped. To strengthen the underdeveloped shield, one cannot simply jump across the Wheel from overdeveloped to underdeveloped. One must move in orderly fashion around the Wheel, first to the adjacent shield. For example, one cannot jump from childhood to adulthood without passing through adolescence. It may be instructive at this point to look at shields that are overdeveloped to add deeper understanding to one's path around the Medicine Wheel.

Overdeveloped Shields[3]

Remember the South Shield is one of "I," body, contests, winning and nothing being enough. The characters in the James Bond movies are caricatures of overdeveloped South Shields. Our emphasis on fitness, thinness, staying young, and being fashionable are other examples. The agony of defeat and the ecstasy of victory are of the South Shield. War, violence, revenge, and genocide are perpetrated by those with a heavy South Shield. When it comes to the natural world and its resources, we and our society have been very much of the "I" and "me" of the South Shield.

---

[3] Gratitude is expressed to Joseph LaZenka of The School of Lost Borders for his teachings on overdeveloped and underdeveloped shields.

With an overdeveloped South Shield, the North Shield is underdeveloped. This means that the sacredness of the "I-Thou" relationship, whether we are in community with another person, state, country, or natural being, does not exist. Thus compromise, cooperation, and mutuality cannot be realized. We have only to look around us at the conflicts in our world to see the evidence of overdeveloped South Shields and the underdeveloped North Shields. Thus we see CEO's and others taking huge bonuses, and for-profit healthcare companies raising rates and earning dollars for investors while the insured struggle to pay premiums or join the ranks of the uninsured.

To achieve balance between the South and North Shields, psyche, whether individual or collective, must move through the darkness and introspection of the West Shield. Reference to the collective here underlines an important concept—the individual person is not the only one traveling around the Medicine Wheel. This model can be applied to tribes, subgroups, nation-states and larger units as well.

An overdeveloped North Shield means an underdeveloped South Shield. The North Shield is about rationality, linear and concrete thinking, organizing, and control. There is no spontaneity or emotion in the North. Mind and science are valued over all else. Everything must be provable or evidence-based. Since the "bottom line" rules, decisions are made without consideration of the impact upon others, especially the natural world and all its beings. Form is worshipped over the spirit.

Again, we do not have far to look to find evidence of an exaggerated North Shield. We can begin with the multinational corporations and the ways in which they have treated both employees and the natural world. We can also look at "No Child Left Behind" in education and the over-emphasis on testing and evidenced-based practice in mental health as overdeveloped North Shield practices. Both attempt to objectively measure us as human beings as if the totality of our being can be measured!

To strengthen the South Shield so as to gain balance, individual and collective psyche must move from the North Shield through the East Shield. Thus one must "let go" of something, allow something to die so that something new can be birthed. Reliance upon rational thinking and science alone must be surrendered. Superiority of one over another must die to have community. Most important, we must let go of the belief that we humans are the center of life and accept our place as being one part of an interconnected Web of Life of which we are but one strand. Without passion and compassion for all, we will not continue to exist.

An overdeveloped West Shield means being lost in the darkness. Magical thinking, depression, and self-loathing are hallmarks. Presenting as a helpless victim, refusing to take any responsibility for the existent situation, and blaming others are characteristics of a person, a community, or country being stuck in the West Shield. Finding it difficult to negotiate relationships with others, the person establishes a relationship with a thing—alcohol, drugs, sex, work, gambling, internet—thus an addiction grows. Despite self-doubt and self-loathing, those stuck in this shield quickly retaliate if they feel threatened then quickly resort to their helplessness when held accountable. Engagement, curiosity, questioning, and self-reflection are blocked by "Why me?" We all know this place well, for going into the darkness to confront one's own darkness is a demanding process. And with reflection, we can also see how communities and nations get stuck in this darkness, too. It is so very difficult to grow into adulthood as a person, a community, or nation-state.

With an overdeveloped West Shield there is an underdeveloped East Shield. The place of light and spirit is weak. The *common ground* of oneness with all things is lacking as is the willingness to see the light in all beings. One cannot find the light without finding the light within oneself. But to get to the east, one must first grow into the maturity of adulthood and find one's place in the community, whether that be personal and professional community, the world of nation-states, or the community of all beings.

An overdeveloped East Shield means an underdeveloped West Shield. Here the person attempts to live in the upper reaches of the spirit world without having found the light by going deeply into the darkness of the west. Here we find the incurable optimist without acknowledging the darkness existent in our own being and that of the world. Enamored of spirit and the New Age, they forget to ask how they might be contributing to events and conditions that trouble them. Again to get to the west, they must travel through the South Shield. They must return to the body, to the senses, to spontaneity, and to play. They must re-find that part that wants to win, that is fierce in their competitiveness, and that is focused on the "I," so that they can free themselves to move into the darkness of their own being in the West Shield.

All of us get stuck at one place or another many times during our repeated passages around the Medicine Wheel. I have been there and you have been there. No judgment or shame can be attached to being stuck. The Medicine Wheel is simply mirroring back information to you and your community. Humility rather than humiliation is what allows one to take the next steps to move beyond one's stuckness. It is both necessary and welcome to have guides, mentors, and teachers to help point the way, support, and encourage. After all, we all have our experiences around the Medicine Wheel and mentoring one another is our gift to the community of all beings. Still, it is for the seeker to take the risk to find what lies beyond and for the community to extend a hand while simultaneously holding accountable those who insist on "I" over "we." At the same time, the "we" must be willing to be introspective, to change, and to grow. Everything is in process, nothing is perfect.

Prelude To Chapters Three Through Seven

The following chapters are set by the Four Shields of the Medicine Wheel. There are stories, reflections, and practices illustrative of each Shield. The stories reflect my own experiences in the natural world and my repeated paths around the Medicine Wheel to a life of growing self-consciousness towards living in peace and harmony. The personal path was not easy nor is it supposed to be. And my path cannot be copied nor is it meant to be. The stories are offerings to others. As offerings they are meant to encourage others to seek and find their *common ground* with the natural world. In so doing, the intention is to help us realize that both our survival and the planet's survival are inseparable.

Categorizing a story in one particular Shield is somewhat artificial for most experiences hold elements of every Shield if change or growth is to occur. It is clear that physical, emotional, psychological, and spiritual growth do not develop in lock-step fashion. Sometimes we are not mindful and we remain stuck in one Shield. We may grow physically and age chronologically while our emotional, psychological, or spiritual development lags. I have organized the stories in this way so that the various practices might reflect significant characteristics of a particular Shield.

Each story is followed by a reflection—a mirror for broadening perspective and creating dialog. At times, a reflection is a musing about "what if." At other times, it mirrors where I am on the Medicine Wheel and the possibility for change and growth. Other times reflections ask hard questions or merely celebrate the journey of life. Regardless of the approach, the reflections are meant to stimulate the reader's musings or those of group members as they reflect upon their own experiences in the world. As such, they are an invitation for continuing the journey around the Medicine Wheel.

Lastly, and most importantly, a number of practices are offered. These are opportunities for the reader, family members, and friends to become seekers and doers by meeting the natural world and allowing it to be the teacher. Thus by becoming active participants, people can continue their own passages around the Medicine Wheel, find one's place in the Web of Life, and discover ways to ensure our and our planet's survival. We are all one.

Though the stories, reflections, and experiences are and will be unique, in sharing them with others we find our *common ground*. Ultimately, the other lives within each of us. Part of the journey is to welcome the other.

The format of the succeeding five chapters is set up to allow the individual reader or leader to approach each chapter as he or she wishes. Some may wish to read all the stories first and then return to reflections and practices. Others may wish to proceed from one set piece to another. A group leader may wish to begin with a practice before returning to story and reflection. In essence, the stories, reflections, and practices are merely tools for seekers and doers to use in ways that are most appropriate for oneself or a group. May you journey well!

CHAPTER THREE

New Beginnings—The East Shield of Birth and Rebirth

Season—Spring
Element—Fire
Color—Gold

Characteristics—birth, rebirth, inspiration, creativity, imagination, enlightenment, mystery, wonder, new beginnings, transformation, trickster, holding both the sacred and the profane

Exaggerated Characteristics—visionary without embodiment, dream with no action, everything is love, head in the clouds

One swallow does not make a summer, but one skein of geese, cleaving the murk of a March thaw, is the spring.
Aldo Leopold in "March" in *Sand County Almanac*

Every time a spirit walks the Earth, a new circle of lessons will be learned in a new body with new understandings.

Jamie Sams and Twylah Nitsch
in *The Council Of All Beings*

West

West Shield of Adolescence

Exaggerated Characteristics:
rebellion, addictions, depression,
self-loathing, victim, self-indulgent

"I am"
consciousness, hero's journey
into change, shadow, self-
introspection, initiation

Characteristics:

South

South Shield of Childhood

Exaggerated Characteristics:
reactive, "I won't grow up!"
"I want it my way!"

Characteristics:
innocence, play, trust,
all senses, body, ego
"I"

North

North Shield of Adulthood

Characteristics:
family, community,
harmony, wisdom, rationality,
action, bringing one's gifts
forward
"We Are"

Exaggerated Characteristics:
overly rational, linear, concrete
focus on mind without feelings

Characteristics:
transformation, birth,
death, rebirth, inspiration,
creativity, spirit, trickster

Exaggerated Characteristics:
visionary without embodiment,
dreams without action, everything
is love

East Shield of Death and Rebirth

Death, Release &
Transformation
Letting Go

East

Blue Road of Death

The East Shield

A GREAT TURNING

Nearing the end of an extended backpacking trip in
Colorado, I am crossing the Continental Divide, the
place where waters flow east to the Gulf and the Atlantic
or west to the Pacific. At 12,000 feet, I am hiking
through pristine alpine tundra. It is early morning, the
air is crisp and clear allowing for dazzling long-distance
views both east and west.

The alpine tundra is a jumble of rocks, watery tarns
and soil for sedges and plant life. The plants are all
miniaturized. Bright yellow faces of alpine sunflowers
turn east to greet the sun. Spectacularly red Indian
paintbrushes stand sentinel-like and catch my eyes
and those of any pollinating insect. Despite the rigor
of surviving at this altitude, life is everywhere. Caught
between the long vistas and the up close and personal,
I drop my pack at trailside to go exploring.

Avoiding the delicate plant life, I hop from rock
to rock, a helter-skelter tour of the tundra. Spiders
scurry over the rocks and grasses—not little spiders
but big ones! There are winged insects. Birds flit about
alternately feeding or rising to float on the breezes. The
shadow of a hawk crosses the landscape. As I prepare
to jump to another rock, a willow ptarmigan suddenly
moves underfoot. In her speckled summer plumage, I
had seen her as just another rock! Startled, I catch my
balance and watch her scurry off while her stone-sized
chicks, similarly dressed, follow her.

Steeped in life, I return to the trail, hoist my backpack onto my shoulders and begin to leave the tundra behind. The terrain now turns to boulders, taller trees, bushes, and plants. An occasional marmot, relative of the eastern woodchuck, whistles an alarm and then runs to hide among the boulders as I approach. Little rabbit-like conies run for cover, too. They survive at this altitude by harvesting, drying. and storing grasses and sedges during this shortened summer season. Small tufts of their harvests lie drying on trailside rocks in preparation for the long winter.

Nearing a rock cairn marking the trail, I see a cony run into the cairn to hide. Then I see a pine marten run up the trail and enter the cairn from the other side. My knowing and reality collide. In the next seconds the air is filled with the agonized screams of the cony. I want to cover my ears, I want to flee; yet I remain rooted to the earth, a helpless witness to the pain and terror of death. Then there is nothing but silence. It is as if the whole world has suddenly stopped—nothing moves. Then the pine marten exits the cairn and runs back down the trail with a limp cony clasped in its jaws. Shaken by the rawness of this meeting, I am fixed here for a long time before I can move on.

A great turning has just taken place—the death of one so that another and its progeny may live.

Reflections

Here was a morning filled with the splendor and vibrancy of life. Suddenly, I am knocked out of my exhilaration. How dare death intrude!

The East Shield holds both life and death. This encounter reminded me that what is here on this planet is all there is and for one being to live, another must die. The cycle of birth, death and rebirth is constant. There are the births and deaths of the mammals, the winged ones, the swimmers, the crawlers, and the trees and plants. Some of the cycles last years and others only days or hours. Often our awareness of this is limited to our gardens, our pets, or our loved ones. Unless we are hunters or gatherers, we are insulated from the death of those beings on whom we depend for our sustenance. Usually we prefer to close our eyes, our ears, and our consciousness to the deaths that surround us daily. It is difficult to hold life and death in the same chalice.

The screams of the cony sent a chill down my spine and rudely awakened me to something I often choose to forget: the cycle of life, death, and rebirth is a constant in my life including my own mortality and that of those I love.

Practices

1) Go out into the natural world and find a being that has died—bird, mammal, tree, plant or other being. Sit with it. Observe its surroundings. Imagine its death. Have a conversation with it. What do you want it to know? What does it want you to know? What is its gift?

2) Go out and harvest something—animal, vegetable, fruit, or tree. What is the place of this being in the circle of life? How might you honor its gift to you? How do you thank Mother Earth, the giver of all life on this planet, for all that she gives to you?

3) Go find a place where waste is collected. What do you see? How do you contribute? Where will this waste go? What will be its impact on the land, air, water and our future resources? Can you do anything to change this?

4) Each life, day, and year has a beginning and an end as does your life. Go out and find a place to watch the sunset. Imagine your own death. How will it be? How would you like people to remember you?

SEEDING

The desert is a strange and foreboding place. Having grown up in the northeast and explored mountains and valleys, the desert is an unknown, yet I am drawn to its starkness and its beauty. Deserts mean creepy, crawly things like snakes and scorpions. Here both to explore my fear and to photograph, I am camping in the high desert of Joshua Tree National Monument in California. It is spring and I am hoping to find a desert carpet of wildflowers. Driving roads from high to low desert and back, I am disappointed to find only the usual blooms of prickly pear, ocotillo, and teddy bear cholla—cacti all efficient at storing water.

Perhaps if I hike into the desert, I may find some hidden oasis, some Garden of Eden. This is scary business, for the desert lacks defined trails like those in the mountains, and it is home to some dangerous creatures, at least from my point of view. There are two possible plans—explore dry washes in the high desert or hike directly into the low desert barren of landmarks to orient me.

Heading to the high desert first, I choose a dry wash and enter in. The deeper I go into this wash, the more confusing it becomes. There are several branches and I am challenged to figure out which is the main branch. Is there a main branch? When I turn around to return to my car will I know which way to go? The sands are indented with the footprints of many wanderers, so much so that I do not know my own boot prints. As if some dark omen, vultures circle endlessly overhead. As I move forward, there is also a part of me that wants to turn and run. Soon I realize there is no oasis and no Garden of Eden. Reluctantly I turn, hoping to follow the right path and find myself back at the trailhead unscathed and sobered.

Having survived this experience, I decide to try the lower desert. Now the challenge is whether I can leave my car, travel cross-country, and return to my car safely. With compass in hand, I set a beeline course from my car out into the unknown. Nervous about getting lost and nervous about meeting a sidewinder, I am hypervigilant. Knowing sidewinders seek sparse shade under scraggly bushes, I give bushes a wide berth! The telltale signs of a sidewinder's travels across the sand simply heighten my anxiety. There are flowers, but I am much too preoccupied with my safety to give them more than passing acknowledgement. Finally, I turn back still with compass in hand and beeline back to my car—a successful compass exercise but not much luck in finding the verdant desert nor in finding peace and harmony!

Reluctantly, I have to admit that this is not the year for desert flowers. The fall and winter rains were insufficient for bringing the desert alive with color. What remains hidden from view are all the tiny seeds hidden beneath grains of sand or caught in crevices and tiny plants—all await next year's rains so that they can burst forth and fill the desert with a miracle of blooms.

Reflections

Desert flowers release thousands of tiny seeds. Some will provide sustenance for small animals and birds. Others will fly on the winds or travel on the coats of animals to land in new territory and await the rains of fall and winter. All of these seeds are filled with the promise of life. Patiently, they await the sweet, life-giving water which will allow them to burst their seed coverings and reach tiny tendrils into the desert earth. Plants emerge, buds form, flowers bloom, winged insects arrive to pollinate, new fruit forms, and the cycle continues.

Isn't this true of us, too? We are both seed catchers and seed sowers. Every day, we seek to catch others' seeds to nurture within us. And, every day as parents, teachers, grandparents, aunts, uncles or friends, we plant seeds. Seeds are ideas, enthusiasms, curiosity, and love. We are the direct link between those who came before us and those who will follow. We open our own fertile ground to grow new seeds. And we sow seeds without knowing which ones will be nurtured into life. It is an act of faith, hope, and love.

Sowing seeds is a tricky business. Encounters are often brief and often we do not know whether the seeds we have sown are nurtured into life or left dormant. All we can do is to freely offer the gift. Until his death at 93, my father spoke fondly of his first grade teacher who rewarded him with a trip to the town library. Living in an immigrant home with no reading materials, he was filled with wonder to step into a room filled with books. This simple act, perhaps given without knowledge of life circumstance, opened a wondrous world to him. He nurtured that gift with a lifetime of reading about nature, geography, travel, and flying—a world that sustained all the years of his life.

Practices

1) In the spring, go sow seeds whether in a plot of land, a pot or roof top garden. Tend your garden. What have you brought to life? Who or what gains from your garden?

2) Who sowed seeds for you? Which ones did you hold onto and nurture? Reflect, are there any seeds you have left dormant and wish to nurture now?

3) Take stock of the seeds that you sow. How do you do that? With whom? How do you feel if the seeds are rejected or left dormant?

4) From where does your faith, hope, and love come?

FIRE AND TRANSFORMATION

With some trepidation I have chosen to hike into and through a fire-burned forest. Last fall flames raced through this National Forest. I have never risked entering such a natural area of death and destruction and I do not know what I will see, hear, smell, taste, or touch. Something draws me to this place yet I feel uneasy entering.

I gather my pack stuffed with lunch, water bottle and raingear, take a deep breath, and step into the unknown. Immediately, I encounter a jumble of lodgepole pine trunks. Some are black and standing while others lean at various angles propped up by blackened sentinels. Then there are those which have already fallen and are dead. In late spring, Forest Service crews sawed through those that block the trail but everywhere else I see a giant "Pick-Up Sticks" world.

Fire is capricious. Some of the trees are totally blackened, others only partially so with some branches still holding brown pine needles. Occasionally, I see a tree that has been entirely spared. When fire invades, it leaps from crown to crown, races across the ground, climbs up the trunks, and travels beneath the ground feeding on the duff and detritus of years past.

Wafts of air carry the aftermath of fire—ash and charred wood. Smell and taste unite. Underfoot there is nothing lush. With each step there is the crunch of seared earth. Occasionally I have to crawl beneath a recent tree fall on the trail.

I have learned that lodgepole pine cones hold onto their seeds until the heat of fire causes them to be released. Eventually the lodgepole forest will return. But I also know that the seeds will need shade and protection in order to sprout. The faster growing aspen seeds will set down roots first, grow, and shelter the slower growing pines. The latter will eventually reach sufficient height to block sun from the aspen which will slowly die and return to earth.

Heartened, I find that despite the blackened trees, the ash, and the dead undergrowth, there are patches of bright green growth that have sprouted up from this devastated earth. Life is already present amidst this destruction. Fireweed with its airy, pink stalks sway in the breeze like flags of hope.

I hear life, too. There are the strident calls of the woodpecker, the first bird to return to the fire zone. Its loud tapping on darkened trunks echoes through the woods. There is the occasional gray squirrel scolding or ground squirrel scampering, harvesting, and planting new seeds. The ruby-throated and rufous hummingbirds hover at the fireweed.

After a few miles, the blackened forest is left behind and I enter an alive and green forest. This was what the fire-burned forest once looked like and will again in the future.

Reflections

This is another East Shield story of transformation. Fire destroys the forest so that new life can take root and wing. For many years, humankind was devoted to preventing forest fires. Remember Smokey the Bear? We did not appreciate fire's role in the health of a forest. Then in the 1980's and 90's we were witness to major fires in our national parks. We learned that in preventing fires the natural cleansing of a forest was interrupted. The accumulated dead trees and plant life on the forest floor simply added more fuel to the fire resulting in conflagrations that took weeks to control. Nature can teach us if we listen.

In the human world, we have embraced fire in symbolic form as a means of transformation. As the sun brings light to the day, fire brings light to the darkness. By shining a light on the darkness, we can give dimension to those things that frighten us. And through the ritual of fire we can symbolically burn some aspect of the self that no longer serves us so that something new can be birthed.

Practices

1) Go out into the natural world and look for signs of death and rebirth. What are the teachings?

2) Think of experiences of endings and new beginnings in your own life. Remember what it

felt like to go through those. Over time, what have you learned about endings and new beginnings?

3) What does it mean when someone says, "When one door closes, another door opens?"

4) We have all experienced many endings and new beginnings. Reflect on those and choose one that seems particularly significant for you.

  a) What did you have to let go of in order to embark on a new beginning?
  b) Was this an easy or difficult letting go? What made it easy or hard?
  c) What did you learn in the process?

5) Think of a decision with which you have been grappling.

  a) What holds you back?
  b) What must you surrender in order to be free to move on?
  c) Write it down. Symbolically let it go by burning it in a fireproof container.

6) At the New Year, reflect on what you would like to let go so that you will be free to embrace something new as the New Year begins. Write it on a piece of paper. Burn it in the fireplace, woodstove or fireproof container.

THE QUICKENING

Spring in the northeast is fraught with promise which is abruptly buried with the arrival of winter's late storms. Anxiously, I await the first signs that spring is here and that we are moving beyond the bone chilling cold and snows of winter. The male red wing blackbirds arrive in March to stake out their territory in the marshes. Usually snow still covers the ground, lakes and ponds lie silent under an icy layer, and more snow will surely come. The earth awakens slowly. On warm days the sap rises unseen in the trees and maple syrup producers begin collecting and boiling off the watery sap to its sweet, syrupy consistency. Lying in bed one morning, I hear the phoebe greeting the dawn with its distinctive call. Spring is coming! On another morning I hear the robin singing and find it sitting high in a tree catching the sun's first rays. These are signs of spring, signs of hope. Still, spring takes its time and despite my longing I cannot rush it along. The buds of the deciduous trees remain tight-fisted. Anxiously, I scan the hillsides for the signs of returning color. Finally around mid-April, a few very warm days arrive and the world quickens. The hillsides redden with the color of maple buds or green-up with expanding birch buds. The warblers arrive as the insects arrive. Black flies hatch. These quicken my pace, too, as I try to avoid becoming their lunch! Then the trees burst forth in delicate flowers and fresh green, miniature leaves. Looking for early spring flowers, I find trilliums, violets, trailing arbutus, and others reaching towards the sky before the shade trees block the sun's warmth. The world is alive with sound and color. What I have longingly awaited has finally come. Then it is over.

Reflections

Spring is the season of unfolding, birth, and transformation. We watch for the first robin, the first crocus, and the first steam rising from the sugar shack. These signs become our touchstones to reassure us that the circle of life continues. We focus on these single markers and are often oblivious to the quiet, even hidden, changes occurring in the earth and its beings. Spring is a process which begins long before the Vernal Equinox and continues into April and May. It is easy to dismiss the process when focused on the goal—the first spring peepers, the eye-catching red tulip, or the smell of lilacs. We cannot feel the earth's warmth below the snow, nor do we see the sap rising, nor do we witness the long migratory flights. What stories the beings in the natural world could tell us about the quickening!

Often in our own lives we get caught up in a goal, pay little attention to the process of getting to the goal, and consequently miss much of our lives. For example, once the prom is over there are only the memories of the night. But what of all the experiences that led up to the prom? What was learned about oneself and others? Or walking across the stage with diploma in hand is a defining moment. But how did you get there? Who paved your way? What did you learn that will sustain you now and in the future? A wedding, a birth, or a death are moments in time. Each is an ending of part of a life-long journey and the beginning of yet another part of the journey. It is important to savor the entire journey, not just the high points. Life's journey takes us around the Medicine Wheel many times. Every circuit is a teacher on our path to peace and harmony.

Practices

1) Plant a garden. When does birth begin? When does the garden move into summer? Nurture and follow it through the seasons. What are its lessons about life, abundance, death, and regeneration? What challenges did you encounter? How did you embrace them? What have you learned?

2) In your yard or in a nearby natural setting, find one being to follow through the four seasons—a tree, a plant, a brook, or some being that will be around all year. Note its changes and moods and your connection to it. You might want to keep a journal of your observations and experiences. What do you learn about change, adaptation, and process? In what ways are you and this being alike? How are you different?

3) If you are approaching a significant life event—change in marital status, significant birthday, change in job, change in health, retirement, or other change in status—reflect upon your path leading up to this

moment. What have you learned about yourself in the process of arriving at this place and time? Where did you get stuck? How did you get unstuck? What do you hope to learn from this next leg of the journey? What would the natural being that you chose to observe in #2 above want to say to you about this change? What would you like to ask it? Have a conversation with this being.

THE TRICKSTER

I am in a Lost Borders workshop entitled Ceremonies
of the Night. I am instructed to go out after sunset and
find a star in the firmament to which to talk. I choose
the North Star for it is known as the star of orientation.
In the Northern Hemisphere it is the one to which
travelers turn to find their way.

Standing in the dark, looking up at the North Star
and thinking about what to say, I request guidance for
the next part of my journey. Suddenly a cloud travels
east and completely obscures the North Star, filling
me with consternation. What do I do now? The cloud
cover is increasing, leaving no hope that the North
Star will reappear this evening. The darkness and
cold penetrate yet I am reluctant to move, even more
reluctant to "fail" in this assignment. Fixed to this spot
and continuing to stare upward into a cloud-filled sky,
a large, winged creature flies from left to right across
the blackness in front of me and disappears into the
night. Shocked, I step backward in surprise and let
out an involuntary "Whoa!" With mind racing, I try
to make sense of what has just happened. I guess
that it may be an owl and begin to hoot hoping for
a response. Of course, nothing responds. Silently I
wait as the cold penetrates deeper into my being.
Minutes pass. Suddenly the creature returns as silently
as before and on the same flight path. Now I can see
its shape more clearly and realize it is not an owl but
a bat! Having had several encounters with small bats

in the Northeast, I am struck by this one's size. With this knowing I am unafraid and instead awed by the experience. What sense am I to make of this? What meaning am I to attach to the disappearance of the North Star and the appearance of bat? Silently I steal away to leave the dark to the bat. Filled with joy and my musings, I begin to sing, softly at first and then more loudly, "We shall overcome, we shall overcome, we shall overcome some day," all the while weeping on my way home. May it be so.

Reflections

This is an East Shield story for two principle reasons. First, the trickster lives in the East. The trickster arrives to help us to let go of something so that something new can be birthed. Just when I think I have something in hand, the trickster comes to turn it all upside down. Dutifully, I am following instructions to find a star but the clouds come to hide it and a bat appears!

Second, I learned early to not trust what I knew, sensed, or felt. Thus my first thoughts are always to rely on someone else for my truth—an adult, a teacher, an expert. Part of my journey has been to know and trust myself.

In the Lost Borders workshop, the trickster challenged me. Where would I go for my answers? I could consult the leaders or others in the group, I could wait until I referred to a book, or I could look inside me to find the teachings of the trickster. In talking to the star, I was looking for guidance, yet the star was hidden by the clouds and bat appeared. What did I know about bat? Bat travels at night, not by its eyes, but by its internal sonar. Ah, I got it! Instead of looking "out there" for my guidance, I needed to look "in here", inside me. I had to let go of my reliance on others to birth a knowing within myself.

I do not know about you, but I realize that the trickster has often shown up in my life when I least expect or want him/her. Filled with anger at being knocked out of my comfort zone, I would spend much of my life fighting against change and transitions. What a colossal waste of time and energy. I am learning that when trickster puts in an appearance, I can let go of some belief, some way of being in the world that will make room for some new way of being.

Practices

1) Think of a question to which you are seeking an answer. State the question. Go out into the natural world and look for a sign that will help you with the answer to your question. Trust your intuition. You will know the sign when you find it. Do not turn away from it. Be with it. What is its message for you?

2) Reflect back on your life. Think about and name a few times when you ignored your intuition. Sometimes it is helpful to think about this as seeing a red flag or seeing flashing red lights at a Railroad Crossing and ignoring either. What caused you to ignore the signs? What did you not want to see or hear? What lessons did you need to learn from these experiences? Have you learned the lessons yet?

3) Again, reflect back over your lifetime. When did the trickster show up? When were you set in your path and confident in your choices and suddenly your life was turned upside down? Did you run away? Did you hold onto old beliefs and patterns? Did you follow a new path? Did you have a choice? Where were you on the Medicine Wheel? What did you learn? Share your story.

4) As we move from an industrial growth society to a sustainable society, many changes will be required of us. Where do you want to be on the Medicine Wheel? Will you wait for the trickster or will you get ahead of him/her? When the trickster makes itself known, how would you like to respond? What are your choices?

No. 15

Several groups of scientists and conservationists are devoted to returning the Whooping Crane to the eastern United States. They have identified a small colony of cranes in northern Wisconsin. A good deal of time, money, energy, and even love have gone into making this project a reality.

When the time for fall migration is at hand, pilots in four lighter-than-air craft shepherd the colony, now grown to 18, to a refuge in central Florida. This year, one of the juveniles, No. 15, has a difficult time staying with the flock on its journey southward. One craft is assigned to remain with No. 15 and to shepherd it to join with the others during rest periods. This is successful until the flock crosses the Georgia/Florida border. At this point, No 15 goes down into a swamp. Despite coaxing, No. 15 refuses to take flight. Not wanting to lose this Whooping Crane, a rescue party is dispatched to capture No. 15, crate it, and transport it to the refuge to join its mates in central Florida. The task is accomplished successfully.

On February 2, 2007, a powerful storm sweeps through central Florida. Strong winds, heavy rains, and tornadoes leave destruction and death in their wake. When the scientists enter the refuge the following day, they find 17 dead Whooping Cranes. They identify each of the cranes by its transponder number and find that No. 15 is the missing bird. They set out to locate the last transponder and the carcass of No. 15. When the team locates the transponder signal, a scientist notes that the signal is not stationary but moving!

Only No. 15 has survived through the day and night. Now it is entirely alone to face the remainder of the season in the South and its preparation for the spring migration northward. Alone it wanders through the refuge until it comes upon a group of Sandhill Cranes. Slowly it joins this community and seems content until the north calls.

Reflections

To me, this is a story of survival, surrender, and acceptance.

The first idea that touches me is that this entire colony, left to their instincts, will fly south not to the eastern United States but to the southwest. They know this through instinct developed through the ages. Yes, through our actions, those Whooping Cranes normally drawn to the southeast have been decimated by loss of habitat, over development, and hunting. So some scientists and conservationists seek to fix what we have wrought as a species. So these birds, whose instinct is to fly to the right, are shepherded to the left. Rather than flying south or southwest, they are pushed east, southeast.

- How many times do we do this not only to other animals but to our own?
- How is it that we get to "know" what is "right" for another?

Actually there are times we do not even care about the other. Instead we are only driven by what we/I want. Everywhere we look, we can find the misuse of power—power designed to enhance one's own power at the expense of others. We see this in the world at large, our own country, in our communities, schools, health care, families, and ourselves.

- How often are we willing to stand in the shoes of the other and feel what it is like?

It is easy to listen to the news of sectarian violence, apartheid, or ethnic cleansing and to be critical of the inhumanity of others; but, how often are we willing to look at that in our own backyard? How often do we commit ourselves to look at our own darkness and to act differently?

The second thing that strikes me is No. 15. On the flight south, it is easy to see No. 15 as weaker than the others. Yet this is the bird that survives while all the others die.

- Why, among the entire colony, does only No. 15 survive especially when it was thought to be weaker?
- Is No. 15 stubborn? Does No. 15 simply fight against the path it is directed to? Or does No. 15 simply surrender to its own path?
- Where is No. 15 during the storm? Where are the others?

- Did No. 15 learn something critical to its survival while living in that swamp on the Georgia/Florida border? Does it know something about survival that the others do not?
- Is No. 15 already an outcast? Or does it simply want to be recognized as a Whooping Crane but a differentiated Whooping Crane?

Often we label those who lag behind or are different as disabled or weaker in some way. And if we cannot find a disabling label then we label as oppositional or defiant. At the same time there is emphasis on both being part of the community and meeting community standards; thus we, metaphorically or really, trap and cage them. When does that cease to serve the person but remain in place to serve the community? How do we know what is "right?"

I am torn. On the one hand, I want to believe in the mystery, that there are no adequate explanations for why No. 15 survived and the others did not. But on the other hand, I also believe there is some larger, universal plan, a spirit that is present.

What I would like to think is that just as all trees are trees, and an ash tree is an ash tree, that when you look closely each tree is a distinct tree unto itself. For each tree, its root system, its shape, the impediments and assets to its growth make each tree an individual unto itself. So it is for No. 15, too. I do not know about its way of being while in the colony in north Wisconsin but I deduce something about its behavior on the flight southeastward. For whatever its spirit, No. 15 was different. The stress of being herded together on the flight created a kind of herd instinct for these Whooping Cranes. I wonder if during the stress of the storm they were drawn together and died together. However, No. 15 found another place in the refuge to outlast the storm. Call it mystery or call it spirit, No. 15 survived.

The third idea is about finding a new home. Yes, Sandhill Cranes and Whooping Cranes are both cranes; but there are differences that have evolved over the eons that make each different from the other. Yet here is a Whooping Crane that has found comfort and contentment with an other.

What is even more striking is that the Sandhill Cranes have accepted No. 15 into their community. The orphan found its way. In not wanting to be alone, it sought community. Two things had to occur. First, the Whooping Crane wanted to not be alone so it went wandering and came upon other birds that had similarities to it. It was juvenile and not driven to power but to community. Second, the Sandhill Cranes accepted No. 15.

I wonder if they are trying to make No. 15 behave like a Sandhill Crane? For now the Sandhill Cranes and No. 15 are content to live side by side. Come spring and the urge to fly north, they may even fly together but at some point No. 15 will seek and find its own kind and the Sandhill Cranes will fly onto their own breeding ground.

- What is it like to be drawn by instinct to move in one direction but to be shepherded in another direction?
- What is it like to live with strangers?
- What is it like to have strangers accept you?
- What does it require to be able and willing to embrace a stranger?

Practices

1) Go out into nature and select some species to study more closely—a certain kind of tree, plant, bird, insect, for example. Look and watch closely. What makes them similar? What makes each different from the other?

2) Now do this in the human world. Select a group and study closely. How are they alike? How are they different? How are they like you? How easy or difficult is it for you to stand in their shoes? Where are you on the Medicine Wheel?

3) If you have an opportunity, watch a small group of newborn or juvenile animals—a clutch of chicks or geese, puppies, kittens, lambs. How do you begin to differentiate one from another? Watch how each grows into its own being.

4) Reflect on a time when you moved into a community of strangers to you—a group, a

dormitory, a work environment, for example. What did the group do to reach out to you and bring you into the group? What did you do to become a member? What did you surrender of yourself? What did you hold onto?

5) Reflect on being a member of a group and having to accept a stranger or newcomer. What did you do to help welcome that person? Did you have to surrender anything to do that?

6) Have you ever been an outcast? What was that like? What, if anything, did you lose during that experience? What might the others have lost? What did you gain? What might the others have gained?

7) Reflect on a time when you were moving along one path in your life and you were drawn to move in another direction—perhaps a major course of study, a career, a partner, a physical move to another part of the country. What decision did you make? Why? What does it require to move into the unknown?

CHAPTER FOUR

Innocence And Trust—The South Shield of Childhood

Season—Summer
Element—Water
Color—Red

Characteristics—childhood, I, ego, innocence, trust, play, emotions, using all senses, Eros, body, magical thinking

Exaggerated Characteristics—reactive, overly emotional, "I want what I want," "I won't grow up," "it won't work," "it's my way or the highway," winning is everything, simplistic thinking, fear

Sultry air hovers, clouds stack heavenward and boomers
    loose rain on a welcoming earth.
Creeks rise to rush beyond their banks then quickly
    fall to being lazy byways.
Breezes redolent with the scents of ripening and harvest
    leave sweetness hanging all about.

Newborns frolic and flit while parents, shepherding
    from a distance, graze and rest.
This is summer—a triumphant symphony filled with
    action and grace.

Anonymous

It is only with the heart that one can see rightly; what
is essential is invisible to the eye.

Antoine De Saint-Exupery in The Little Prince

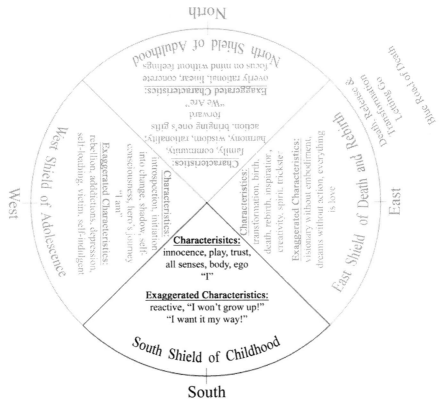

North

North Shield of Adulthood

Exaggerated Characteristics:
overly rational, linear, concrete
focus on mind without feelings

"We Are"

Characteristics:
family, community,
harmony, wisdom, rationality,
action, bringing one's gifts
forward

West Shield of Adolescence

West

Exaggerated Characteristics:
rebellion, addictions, depression,
self-loathing, victim, self-indulgent

"I am"

Characteristics:
introspection, initiation
into change, shadow, self-
consciousness, hero's journey

Blue Road of Death

Death, Release, &
Transformation
Letting Go

East Shield of Death and Rebirth

East

Exaggerated Characteristics:
visionary without embodiment,
dreams without action, everything
is love

Characteristics:
transformation, birth,
death, rebirth, inspiration,
creativity, spirit, trickster

Characterisitcs:
innocence, play, trust,
all senses, body, ego
"I"

Exaggerated Characteristics:
reactive, "I won't grow up!"
"I want it my way!"

South Shield of Childhood

South

The South Shield

PLAYING

During the latter part of childhood, I live on a farm. Drawn to the woods and stream that cover the northern end of the property, I often go exploring and take great pleasure in trying to be as silent as I can while walking through the woods, always on the lookout for animals.

One late and sunny afternoon, I steal away to the woods looking for adventure. Not far in, I hear the rustling of old leaves and ground cover just beyond a small knoll. Filled with anticipation, silently I creep forward. There they are! Two young raccoons tumbling and wrestling, and I sense the mother is not far away. I hold my ground in wonder and joy. Animals play, too! Being witness to this encounter brings me still closer to the natural world and fuels future explorations.

As I move more deeply into the natural world, I witness more play. I know that play is the practicing of the skills necessary for survival but sometimes, I think, it is for the pure pleasure of being alive.

- On a canoe trip in northern New Hampshire, a friend and I watch two young bear cubs shepherded by their mother. They are romping through the woods and chasing up and down trees with such apparent glee and freedom. They wrestle and scamper while mom strolls along behind. We are filled with the excitement of being witness to this. We are on the other shore of a small cove picking and eating wild raspberries while watching these antics. But wait! They are heading around the small cove to the very berry patch we are enjoying! Quietly, we retreat to our canoe and leave the berries to them while taking with us a delightful memory.

- Oftentimes on mountain tops I find myself watching crows or ravens playing with the wind. They climb, spread their wings, and allow the wind to blow them to another place in the sky. Other times they climb high, then pull their wings tight against their bodies, and dive fast into the valleys only to climb again and repeat this maneuver. Earthbound as I am, I watch with a mixture of exhilaration and jealousy. How wonderful it would be to fly, soar, and dive with such abandon! Then one day while driving to work, I watch a crow flying down the road's path displaying all the usual aerial antics. Then suddenly, the crow rolls over and flies upside down. I laugh with joy. Pushing the limits extraordinaire!

- Then I have seen otters in the winter sliding down snow mounds in a brook, diving into the water, exiting to slide down yet another mound. Their playful freedom is to be admired.

- Have you watched new born foals discovering what they can do on their unsteady legs? Soon they are romping, chasing, and flying across the pasture!

- Perhaps the funniest scene I have ever witnessed was watching cows running and leaping in a pasture after a winter locked in a barn. Cows, these big hunks of flesh and bone, jumping, kicking, slipping, sliding, racing, and feeling space and air above and below. The earth trembles beneath their hooves. Their excitement at being free produces pure abandon. One, finding a weak place in the fence, plunges through to still greater freedom and all follow. Now I know how cows can jump over the moon!

Reflections

As we move from childhood to adolescence to adulthood, our lives become so much more constricted and serious. How unfortunate we leave behind the joy, the spontaneity, and pure pleasure of the freedom of play. Our collective view of adulthood is so rooted in the North Shield that we do not allow ourselves to play with abandon. We are afraid to be laughed at, to be considered childish, or to be scorned. Not only do we leave play behind but we jettison it and look down upon it to claim our adulthood. Yet play is as important a foundation of our being as any dimension of life. It is a necessary element of creativity. It is a necessity for spontaneity, freedom, joy, and an expanded sense of self. Play allows us to push the limits, to feel the exhilaration of walking the edge, and to be fully alive. It feeds the spirit.

These experiences in the world of nature bring me to life. They remind me to laugh, to lighten up, to play, and to recapture the spontaneity and creativity of childhood. They carry me around the circle.

Practices

1) Take a child with you into the natural world. Get down and dirty and experience the world from his or her level. Be curious with him or her. Let the child teach you how to play. The only rule is to do no harm.

2) Go out into the natural world and find the child within you. Re-member what you did as a child. Climb a tree, float sticks down a stream, frolic in fall's leaves, play in the mud, build a snow being. Pay attention to what you must let go of to fully move into the experience.

3) Go into the natural world and find a young being to watch and study. Experience the world at hand from this being's perspective. What must it learn in order to grow into adulthood? What qualities will it be necessary to have in order to accomplish this? Which of these qualities do you already possess? Which have fallen into disuse? Which ones do you need to support anew or relearn?

4) In community, take on the role of a being from the natural world. Create something which will identify you to the others in the community. Play out your roles for a planned amount of time. What did you learn about that being through your play? What did you learn about yourself? What did you learn about others? Come together to share this experience. What is the learning from this community sharing?

A SENSE OF WONDER

Going out to the pasture to bring the cows in for milking, riding high on a big red tractor, finding a fox's den, catching a wriggling fish at the end of a homemade fishing pole—these are fond memories of the four-year-old me with my father and his brother on the farm my uncle managed. The excitement of adventure beyond the house's four walls left me begging to go with them anytime they left, making me the ever-present tag-a-long. Beyond the adventure, what I recall most keenly were their smiles, their joy in my joy. Little wonder that explorations in the world "out there" came to hold such pleasure and significance for me. That same joy in others' joy has allowed me to share the natural world with many.

- I am an assistant in a Nature's Classroom with a group of fifth graders and we are exploring the edge of a fresh water pond. With white porcelain pans, we are collecting water and detritus to find what lies hidden. Life emerges from what looks dead and rotting. The children are excitedly exclaiming about the crawling and squiggling creatures in the bottom of the pan. We study with a magnifying glass, draw pictures, and consult a guide book to identify these living creatures. Moving from the pond's edge to a stream, carefully we begin turning over stones to find what lives beneath. A crayfish scurries to hide elsewhere. There are excited shouts. Later, we return to our cabin tired, wet, muddy, happy, and with new eyes that look beyond the surface.

- Another adult and I are leading eleven middle school boys and girls on a six-week, cross-country camping experience. These are teens of urban and suburban life and most have had very little experience of responsibility for themselves or to others. The challenges are many—learning to set up a tent, cooking meals for thirteen, keeping gear organized, and being packed and ready to load the van at the agreed upon time. There is little time for wonder when these skills need to be learned. As we make our way west, they become more adept and can find time for a sense of wonder—hiking to a hidden, iced-in lake; catching sight of mountain goats; meeting a doe; watching a Kingfisher kill a fish before swallowing it; and coming upon a moose cow and newborn calf. These middle schoolers are old enough to learn and young enough to be stunned into silence.

- A small group of college students and I are on a weekend backpacking trip in Vermont. We are on a circle route that will take us up a mountain ridge then down to a backcountry lake and then out via a lowland trail. This is a new experience for these urban dwellers willing to engage the unknown. It is early spring, the snow is finally gone but the trail is muddy. It is partly sunny and there is a nip in the air. By noon, we gain the top of the ridge and climb a fire tower. Looking out over the landscape, a young man exclaims about being as high as the clouds and the wonder of seeing the shadows of clouds cast upon the land below. Suddenly a new dimension is added to his life. How simple a concept but so easily missed without a mountain experience.

Reflections

The South Shield is not only about the self, I, and ego; it is also about the innocence, trust, and wonder of childhood. There is a necessity for an "I" before one can open to new experiences and the willingness to find life beyond "I." How often we live flat lives. How often we treat the world around us as the same old, same old. How do we make the world multidimensional? When do we really look and really see? In moving out of the environment with which one is familiar, one's senses can be awakened.

I chose these three anecdotes to reflect different ages. The fifth-graders are ten years old and on an Outdoor Education week. For many this is their first experience in a camp setting. They are not squeamish but trusting and curious. When they look at pond water expecting to see nothing and discover life, they begin to look more closely. Their energy increases, their enthusiasm grows as does their curiosity. The middle school group of thirteen- to fourteen-year-olds struggle with identity and belonging. Their energy is focused on self and how to connect with the others all of whom are strangers. What they say and what they do are often at odds. The challenge for me is to not be turned off by their self-centeredness but to find ways to pique their curiosity while focusing on what they say, not what they do. As for the college-aged students, the young man was not the only one who had never been that high before but he was the only one who risked allowing his surprise to be given voice. He could still be fascinated and captured by wonder.

Practices

1) Go out and find the child in you. What are the gifts that your child part brings forth?

2) Do something new in the outdoors, something you have not done before and bring your curiosity and innocence with you:

   • walk a familiar path at a snail's pace
   • visit a previously unexplored area or trail
   • study a one-yard square piece of earth
   • walk in a light rain
   • take a night walk and listen to the night sounds
   • lie on the earth
   • crawl into a cave

- climb a tree
- hug a tree
- hold a living creature

3) Do any of the above with a child and let their enthusiasm, innocence, and trust catch you.

EGO AND RACCOON

I grew up on stories of heroes. The books I read were the classics as well as stories of those who ventured into the unknown and survived. Westerns were popular in both the movie theaters and, later, on television. So, of course, there were the cowboy revolvers and cap guns and, when we moved to the farm when I was ten, there was first a BB gun and then a .22 rifle, both used for target practice.

On a poultry farm, raccoon and fox are natural predators. The raccoons were numerous and many mornings we would go out to the hen yard and find a dead or dying hen. My father would trap the raccoons then kill them, or sometimes he would bait them with a live chicken and shoot them. Often I would go with him on these nighttime outings of bait, wait, and shoot. The wait was usually boring and I would fall asleep lying on the ground, only to be jolted out of my sleep with a loud BANG as the gun went off beside my head!

It is mid-afternoon and my sister, brother and I are walking up our lane after school. Talk is always sparse amongst us so I am usually looking into the woods to see what I can see. On this afternoon I see a raccoon sitting in the crotch of a tree. Dashing home, I breathlessly tell my mother about the raccoon and beg her to let me take the .22 rifle to kill this denizen of the hen yard. She is reluctant, but I am both persistent and convincing, and she gives in to my pleadings. Knowing where the rifle and ammo are kept, I retrieve them, and we all troop back to the killing ground. Filled with excitement and thoughts of success that will make my father proud of his teaching and my skill, I relocate the raccoon, load a single bullet, aim, pull the trigger, and miss—but I am close. The raccoon is stirred to action and prepares to retreat down the tree. Reloading and making my correction, I squeeze the trigger, the raccoon is hit, and falls dead from the tree, and I am the Great Hunter! Tying a rope around one of its hind legs, I carry the raccoon back to the house and nail the carcass to the garage door. It will be the very first thing my father will see when he turns for the garage. With barely controlled anticipation, I listen for his car and ready for a celebration. He enters from the garage and asks about the raccoon, and I recount my deed—my contribution to saving the hens. He says nothing and sits down for dinner.

Reflections

As I reflect back on this experience, I am struck by several reactions. First, this is a South Shield story. It is a story about ego, about my needing recognition, and about my living out the stories of heroes. How desperately I was trying to define myself through the eyes of my father, to no avail. Failing once again to please him, my anger turned inward.

Second, I am astounded by the complete disconnect between that part of me that took such joy in exploring the woods—listening and looking for raccoons and other wildlife just to be pleasured by the sight—and that ego-driven part of me out to kill. That part was driven by family and farm. The raccoon was killed for what it might do in the future, and for what I needed from my father. The ego pulls us away from the present moment and away from who we are at core.

Third, this story is repeated in the middle of my adult life when I am living in Vermont. While studying photography and working part-time, I am renting a room from an eighty-year-old widow. Over time we became close friends and I loved living in this old farm house and helping out with chores. One of the things I loved doing was helping to plant and nurture the vegetable garden. Each morning we both took pleasure in weeding, hoeing, watering, and admiring the daily transformation. Then one day we went out and the lettuce was gone and the broccoli heads had disappeared! Annoyed but wiser in years, my friend took a judicious view in figuring ways to stop the family of woodchucks that had invaded. So we put up fencing, hung white strips of rag, sank the fencing into the ground—all to no avail. In the meantime, I was filled with consternation. How dare woodchucks invade "our" garden! In desperation, my friend relented to gassing the woodchuck burrow. That did not work for they simply exited through one of their escape routes. The garden was slowly being depleted and the woodchucks were getting fat at our expense! Then I found she still had her husband's old .22 rifle and I set about being "our" garden's protector. Possessiveness begets ego and ego begets possessiveness.

BANG! The bullet hit flesh with a dull thud and I felt revulsion; but I continued my daily slaughter until the entire woodchuck family was gone. Not having the stomach for dragging off carcasses, I left that task to the garden's owner.

Fourth, I am struck at how the ego does not want to look at its work. My ego does not want to consider the aftermath of my deeds. It would like me to keep the raccoon or woodchuck as "other" not as a being just like me. We wonder from afar how torture, rape, and killing can happen in the world. We judge, yet everyday ego brings us to our knees as human beings.

Practices

1) Reflect on a time in the natural world when your ego led you to act in a way that you now regret. What was the cost to you? What was the cost to the natural world? Is there a way that you might repair that now? If so, do it.

2) Reflect on a time in the world of human beings when your ego led you to act in a way that you now regret. Sit with the one you hurt or maimed. In reflection, how were you alike? How were you different? What would you like to say to that one now?

3) Reflect. Whose life have you taken recently? For what purpose? How was it accomplished? How do you make it right with the universe?

4) In the indigenous way, all beings are honored—animal, vegetable and matter. Most of us are far removed from the beings we consume. Try growing something in a container—herbs, tomatoes, lettuce. When you harvest it, honor its being, its contributions to you and its place in the circle of life. Even if you are not the harvester, how do you honor those beings that sustain your very being?

5) What has ego led us as a people to destroy? Begin with other two-leggeds and then move on to other parts of the Web of Life. What do we need to do to change this? What can you do?

ME FIRST

I am house- and pet-sitting for dear friends of mine. This is of mutual advantage, for I will be free to write and the family pets and house will be safe and secure and well cared for. This seems idyllic to me. The house overlooks the water. There is a deck and chairs, a screened porch, and many creature comforts. The pets arc two cats, five chickens, and a goose. This is the daily pet care routine:

A.M. rising

- feed each cat at separate stations in the kitchen, one gets half of its a.m. allotment of dry food, the other one teaspoon of canned cat food
- freshen water both inside and outside
- let cats outside—throughout the day, they come and go as they please
- replenish fresh water for chickens and goose and replenish food, if needed
- let chickens and goose out of hen house but keep penned

Mid-morning

- feed one cat medicine pill wrapped in canned food
- open pen so that chickens and goose can roam freely

Noon

- feed one cat remainder of a.m. dry food

Late afternoon

- feed each cat p.m. food allotment, again giving only half of dry food to one cat
- keep cats inside now
- close chickens and goose in pen and spread some corn for them

Dark

- close chickens into the hen house
- feed cat remainder of p.m. food

If needing or wanting to go to town, I must leave the fowl penned with a cracked corn treat. This way they will be safe from predators. And one of the cats should be inside since she would be sorely challenged to escape a predator. There are predators in this area. One day a fisher took one of the geese despite the owners' efforts to drive it away.

Usually the rhythms of the day reflect my rhythms. Instead I find myself watching the clock, organizing my time around the animal schedule and needs, and finding it difficult to settle into writing. After a few days of this, a dis-ease sets in. While feeling annoyed at having to set my schedule to the animals, I am also feeling guilty about my resentment since this opportunity was offered to me as a gift. After all, here is a vacation and time to write for little financial cost.

Reflections

Here I am, stuck in the South Shield, the place of "I", certainly not the place of "we." But to get to "we", I must move through the West Shield, the place of "I am" and "you are." This is a stunning realization for me while I also see it as reflective of our culture. In so many ways, we are self-serving. We think about ourselves first and others later. Here they are, animals, beings on this planet, totally dependent upon me for their care and safety, and I am resentful! Here I am writing about living in harmony with and honoring all beings on the planet and I am resentful about setting my rhythms to their needs! At the same time I like their companionship. The cats purr and want to spend the evenings with me. The clucking and scratching of the hens remind me about growing up on a farm. The goose's antics in its rush to freedom are laughable.

Me-first attitudes pervade our planet—economically, politically, communally, and individually. I am chagrinned to meet my selfishness and wonder where else it shows up? It reminds me about how important it is to live with consciousness every moment. When I am able to live with conscious intent, I have more opportunities to travel around the Medicine Wheel. It reminds me again that life is a journey, community is hard to achieve, and that ego is a trickster.

Practices

1) Think about all the decisions you make that are self-serving without regard to the cost to others and to the planet. Some thoughts:

   • Which trips are really necessary?
   • Do you purchase items produced by sweatshop labor?
   • Do you purchase products in which the grower or creator does not receive fair market remuneration?
   • Do you recycle?
   • When you are cold, do you put on another layer or turn up the heat?
   • When you are hot, do you turn on the air conditioner or take other steps to be cool?

   a) Choose one of your decisions. How could you do it differently? Do it.
   b) Choose one that you feel you cannot change because of time, money, energy, or desire. What can you do to pay back to the planet?

2) When and where does your selfishness show? Why does it appear? What can you do differently? What do you need in order to accomplish that?

BLIND FEAR

I have a permit to backpack a forty-mile circle route in Yosemite from Tuolumne Meadows, down into the Hetch Hetchy, and back to Tuolumne. The guide book indicates that rattlesnakes are plentiful in the Hetch Hetchy area deep in the canyon. Having sent for my permit in January when New Hampshire is buried deep in snow and cold, I spent no time worrying about rattlesnakes other than to say to myself, "I'll deal with it."

Now I am in the sixth day of my trip and I am descending a trail that will take me to the depths of the Hetch Hetchy. It does not help that I am in a thunderstorm with cracks of lightning shaking my bones. As I descend further into the canyon, my fear rises. The deeper I go, the greater the fear that I will run into a rattlesnake. Despite my attempts, there is no running away from the terror that grips me. Feeling trapped, I realize there is no escape. Retracing my steps is out of the question for that will take me six days. There is no one to "rescue" me. Arriving at the camping area, I set up my tent in the very center of the largest open area in hope that rattlesnakes will not venture across the expanse. Uneasy, I do not stray far. Looking around carefully, I am nervous each time I leave my tent. Part of me is embarrassed at being so afraid. It is my "internalized other" judging me. But the terror is real and I cannot push it away. My only question is, "How quickly can morning come so that I can escape this place?"

Sleep is fitful and with first light I am out of my tent and packing up. I am anxious to leave this canyon and hope that with nightfall I will be free of rattlesnake country. Ever vigilant, I hoist my pack, cross the open expanse, and arrive at the trail only to find it completely overgrown with foot high grasses! Fear grips my stomach for I imagine snakes hiding in the grasses. How am I going to do this? Obviously I cannot stay here, yet I am terrified to take one step forward. I must go forward. I have no choice. Holding my backcountry ski poles out in front of me, I plow the grasses aside and step forward onto the trail. I hike on, with my eyes ever-vigilant but my mind detached.

My fear does not subside but merely becomes something to be endured until I escape the canyon and the rattlesnakes. Leaving the grasses behind and hiking up a rocky, dusty trail, I expect a rattlesnake at every turn—beneath a ledge, curled up on the side of the trail, ready to strike. What suddenly flashes in my mind are my recurring dreams of having to cross an area swarming with snakes. The memories become my companion and make the day all that more difficult. Rattlesnakes never show themselves, but there is no relief, for by the end of the day I realize I have not left rattlesnake territory behind. I still have a half day tomorrow. Mentally exhausted, this trip ceases to be fun. I cannot wait to be out of here.

Arising early the next morning, packing quickly and heading out onto the trail, I finally gain the forest by late morning—a place of coolness, shade, and no rattlesnakes!

Relief should be at hand. Instead I feel nothing. There is still another night before I end this trip.

On the last morning I am hiking through high mountain meadows. This is one of my favorite places to be on Earth, yet something is not right. Though I never met a rattlesnake, some part of me was lost in the canyon.

Reflections

This fear put me fully in the South Shield of childhood. How I wished I could be rescued or that I could magically transport myself out of the canyon into a place of safety. I felt so little and powerless.

This fear was all too familiar to me. Feeling trapped in the canyon, all I could do was to push forward. That was a coping skill that I developed early in my life. How interesting that it took this wilderness experience to bring this to my conscious mind. During that trip, my fifty-something body was carrying not only my backpack but a terrified child. Her appearance surprised me. She brought home to me a part of me I had hidden away. She reminded me of how many times in her young life she had been terrified and, with no sources of safety, had to "put on blinders" to block the fear so as to survive. To escape the canyon, I had to put the terror someplace so I could act. It took me three months back in New Hampshire before I was more centered and more fully back in my body. Some coping skills come with great costs.

Fears can paralyze us and stunt our growth, especially if an experience which causes fear is beyond our ability to cope in healthy ways.

Fear can be an important teacher. Usually we do not enjoy feeling out of control. We may have been taught to be ashamed of our fears. Then we learned to fear not only the judgment of others but also our judgment of ourselves. Our fears have the power to keep us from growing. Instead of denying or avoiding our fears, what would happen if we allowed our fears to be our teachers?

Practices

1) Name three things in the natural world of which you are afraid. Choose the one that is least frightening. How might you take the power back from this fear? Desensitizing is one way to meet a fear. This entails taking small steps first in your mind and then in the real world. Meet the fear in controlled settings so that you can easily disengage if your fear becomes unmanageable.

2) Name three fearful situations you have met in the human world—a job interview, traveling alone, learning to drive, or first day of school or a job. For each, how did you negotiate this experience? What helped you? Did anyone help? What did you learn that you used in future situations?

3) We may never recover fully from some fears. Many of us live with differing levels of Post-Traumatic Stress Disorder. Many are war veterans, first responders, accident victims, crime victims, or victims of abuse or neglect.

a) Where do you find safety in the world?
b) What healthy techniques have you developed to soothe yourself?
c) With whom do you share your fears?

LETTING GO

Having registered for a day-long rock climbing class, I am driving to the Schwangunk Mountains in New York State's Catskills. Since I have a fear of heights, I am not really sure why I am doing this. What am I out to prove? Fearing the siren that will lure me to jump into space, I do not climb fire towers and I keep clear of precipices. Nevertheless, here I am. I arrive at the crude parking area, meet the instructor and the other students. Of course, I am nervous and spend much of my time watching and trying to figure out if and where I will fit in. The instructor unloads all the equipment and asks us to gather it up—ropes, slings, pitons, carabiners, along with our bag lunches and water bottles—and walk through the woods to the base of a cliff. Laden down with gear, we dutifully march into the woods complete with the musical sounds of clanking metal gear. Arriving at the cliff face, we drop the gear and our lesson begins. We learn how to tie into the rope and, in my nervousness, I am all thumbs. "Let's see, the rabbit goes around the tree, then down the hole and then what?" With practice, I get it. Next is the etiquette of climbing and how to belay from below. We practice the skills with our feet planted firmly on Mother Earth. There is a rhythm to how the rope is played out or gathered in, and that requires coordination between my two hands. I am concentrating hard. If I am going to be responsible for someone at the end of the rope, I do not want to mess up. He is depending on me. The next part of the lesson focuses on the art of climbing—maintaining three points of contact with the rock while the fourth point (hand or foot) seeks a new toe or hand hold, maintaining one's center of gravity over the feet to prevent slipping, and taking time to move in a planned and deliberate way. This the instructor demonstrates while we watch and then he sends us out to try some bouldering—moving up and down boulders while remaining close to the ground. With a little practice, I am learning what the soles of my boots can do on rock, how much grip they give me, and how not to lean too far forward and slip downward.

Now we are ready to attempt the rock face. The leader climbs with a bottom belayer. The climber sets a piton, slips a carabiner through the hole in the piton and then the rope into the carabiner. In this fashion he completes the first pitch, finds a place into which he ties for safety, and then top-rope belays each of us in turn. I hang back to watch, to commit to memory the procedures, and to gather my nerve. Finally I step forward to be the third climber. I tie into the rope and check the knot. The first step is daunting for it requires a big reach with each hand and a big step up. Being shorter than the others, I am at a disadvantage. The only woman in the class, I want to be smooth about this, but instead I stumble and clamber my way past the first hurdle! So much for grace! But once past this, the remainder of the climb is surprisingly easy. The top-rope belay affords a measure of security. It is a life-line to another human being. Not only does it keep me from falling should I slip but it also silences any siren call. Totally present in the moment, I leave the bonds of Earth to confront my fears and test my courage.

There are two more pitches, each of 100 feet or so. My fear subsides with each pitch. Finally we attain the top of the ridge, stop to eat lunch, and rest. Everyone seems to relax. Having reached the top, we must now descend by rappelling. The belayer, the instructor, ties into a sturdy tree. Then he explains how to wrap the climbing rope around one's body using it as a brake as we descend back to Earth. Though the belay rope, the second rope, is a safety, the rappeller is in complete control of the speed of descent by allowing the climbing rope to slip through one's steadying hand while the other hand controls the speed of the descent by creating or loosening the friction of the rope around one's body. There are warnings about not letting go and not going too fast because friction causes burns to the hands or body! The instructor asks for the first volunteer.

Now my fear has returned only in double strength. One thing I have learned is that if I wait too long, the fear overrides and I become unable to act. Sometimes it is far easier for me to get to what lies beyond fear— relief—so I volunteer. For me, this is a huge test in "letting go"—letting go of fear, distrust in myself and another, and the bonds of Earth. To descend, I must lean back over nothingness until my body is at a forty-five degree angle to the rock face. Slowly, very slowly, I lean back but grip the rope too hard and remain stuck, then let go too much and lurch backward. In this jerky manner, I begin walking down the face of the cliff while playing out the rope trying to maintain that forty-five degree angle. Then I reach an overhang and lose contact with the rock. Now I am swinging and twisting completely free of the rock. Surprised, I realize my safety is entirely wrapped in these two ropes. There is nothing to do except to continue to play out the rope, my only tether to the Earth. When my boots finally touch the Earth, I call, "off belay." Anxiety and fear are replaced by huge relief and satisfaction. But at the same time, there is a touch of sadness. I want to go back up and "let go" again!

Reflections

This story can be placed in various shields but I chose to put it in the South Shield as an example of letting something die so that something new could emerge. This was my first experience in confronting my fear of heights and a fear that I would be drawn to my death. I have no clear recollection of the source of these fears. I do remember being stuck up a tree I had climbed when I was little. It had been much easier to ascend than to descend. Quickly, I learned that I needed a plan for both the way up and the way down! But this did not seem to be a significant source of my fears. In fact these fears did not seem to be based in fact but were irrational fears.

Before I confronted these fears, I had had many experiences of solo hiking and backpacking. In other words, I had gone around the Medicine Wheel many times releasing other fears—fear of the darkness, of being alone, of getting lost—before I confronted this fear.

Over the years, this is what I have learned. My anticipatory anxiety controls me and gets in the way of living in the present moment, the NOW. Of what am I afraid? When I need to be in control of myself and my environment I limit myself. The reality is that I cannot control my environment in the human world or in the natural world. I can be in control of the challenges I accept, and I can be in control of how I choose to respond.

I have also learned that I can trust my ability to respond, but to grow more fully into my wholeness, I must "show up." Showing up has three components—preparation, action, and incorporation. First, I must prepare myself by taking on a challenge that is within my capabilities. For example, in rock climbing, routes are graded by degree of difficulty. To maximize my experience, I want to attempt a route that will challenge, not bore me. This would be a route that will require me to stretch my skills, yet its degree of difficulty will not be so great as to overcome me with anxiety and failure. This happened to me the first year of downhill skiing. Having practiced basic skills on beginning trails, I took the lift to the top of the mountain. As I gazed down the mountain, I will never forget the fear rising in the pit of my stomach. These trails were way beyond both my skill and my confidence. What was I thinking? Why did I let myself get talked into this? Somehow I got down the mountain, obviously with many falls, but I never returned to downhill skiing. Never did I want that feeling again.

Second, after committing to the challenge appropriate to my abilities, I must give myself fully to the challenge. I cannot undertake this in a half-hearted manner. Actually, the act of commitment transports me to the "in-between time," that liminal space to which I surrender—the stepping off or the leaping forward and trusting that I will "land" safely—thus successfully meeting the challenge. When I trust myself, I can give myself fully to the experience and live in the present moment.

Third, I must bring the learning into my being. Learning occurs at a variety of levels—physically, emotionally, psychically, and spiritually—and to fully incorporate the experience, I need to consciously internalize it. You will note that I have not said anything about successful completion of the goal. Not all goals are met; for example, a climb aborted due to weather or a backpacking trip cut short by bears, injury, or misjudged skills. What is important is the process, not the goal. Every experience brings its learning. It is this learning that must be incorporated.

When I let go of what holds me back, a small death occurs so that I may be transformed and learn to let go again and again. This is what allows me to travel ever around the Medicine Wheel.

Practices

1) We all have dreams. Make a list of the things you would like to do but are afraid to attempt.

   a) For each, list the fears that stop you.
   b) Choose one of those dreams. Make a list of the steps that you might take that could bring you closer to realizing this dream. Consider the resources that you might consult to help you with your dream. This is preparation. Now act!
   c) Now incorporate this experience into your being. What did you learn about yourself? What did you learn about your environment? Does this free you to try something else? If so, what might you try next?

2) Think of something you would like to do in the natural world but cannot because of your fear. What steps could you take that could get you closer to your goal? For example, going out into the natural world alone and at night for two hours. Hint: Sit on the steps of the porch with a light on, then without a light, then move a chair into the yard, move to the edge of the woods, etc.

3) Each of us has entered the unknown many times in our lives. Just remember—first days of school or summer camp, first date, first dance, traveling alone, and so on. What qualities did you need to rely upon to accomplish these "firsts"? What did you need from others? What did you learn about yourself in the process? What did you learn about the world?

LEARNING TO TRUST

It's an early morning in June 1968. I awake to the morning news. The somber voices alert me to tragedy. It is just a few months after the assassination of Martin Luther King. Listening with a mixture of dread and curiosity, leaden voices announce that Robert F. Kennedy has been killed after winning the California Democratic Presidential Primary. An ache of despair and grief begins in the pit of my stomach and fills my body. What is happening to us? I had held such hope for his candidacy.

I am in my late 20's which is old by the standards of the young people of the 60's but I am very young in other ways. In the 60's, people come together to protest but few come together to grieve. In my isolation, I am left trying to figure out what to do with my despair. I do not feel angry but I am worried about us as a nation. Candles, marches, and flowers are not common expressions of grief, yet I feel I must do something to honor this man and his ideals. The community of church is foreign to me so that is not an option. I am thinking that I should perform some sacrifice. But what? Pondering this for three days, I can think of little. Finally on Friday evening I decide I will hike to the top of Whiteface Mountain in New York State's Adirondack Mountains. I awake early the next morning, pack a day pack, and drive north thinking I "should" do this but not feeling very energetic.

I drive to the trailhead and head out onto the trail. It is a warm, sunny day, the trail is dry with no running water, and the black flies are out and about. The trail climbs steadily. There is nothing that feels good about this hike. There is no joy. This feels like a forced march, yet I remind myself that this has been my commitment—to hike to the summit. A silent war grows within me. It is a war of "should" versus "could". My head tells me to trudge on to fulfill the commitment, while my heart tells me I could turn back. My ego tells me I am a quitter if I turn back. I also worry about what others will think if they know I quit. I know my heart is not in this endeavor. There is something that does not ring true but I cannot put my finger on it. Still, I trudge on carrying this internal battle with me. Over and again, I ponder going forward or turning back, and struggle with all the rational and irrational reasons for doing either. Usually energized by hiking, I find that I am stopping frequently not so much from physical fatigue as from the emotional exhaustion of struggling with a decision. Finally, an hour into the hike, I turn back never to return to this mountain.

Reflections

Oh, the South Shield! This was not an easy decision for me to make. I was young and immature in many ways. Usually my decisions were made based on what others wanted or thought. To please and to maintain connection was what I was taught. I was also taught not to be a "quitter." Quitting brought shame for giving up. How deeply these beliefs were embedded in my psyche is clear. Here I am out in the wilderness totally alone yet captive to what others may think, and captive to my own internalized self-hatred. It took courage to turn around. In doing so, I was willing to enter the West Shield to confront my own darkness and to find grace in my decision.

How do we know when to push on and when to turn back? Where am I on the Medicine Wheel if I trudge on? What motivates me—guilt, shame, ego, self-hate? Where am I on the Medicine Wheel if I turn back? Why? Is there a way to hold either choice without judgment? If so, where would I be on the Wheel?

Every day we are faced with many choices—to say "yes", "no", or "maybe"; to go or stay; to obey or disobey; to take responsibility or to blame; to be silent or to speak out. How we go about making these decisions tells us where we are on the Medicine Wheel. Does our power lie within or without? How do we decide? Every choice we make has its gains and its losses. There is no perfect decision. In turning back, I had to come to peace with myself. I had to struggle with my concepts of failure and success. In growing, I had to be willing to leave something behind, not with bitterness or judgment, but with a clear acknowledgement that what had served me well for some time was no longer needed in this situation. I would pass through the South Shield again many times in the future as I struggled with bringing my head and heart into alignment and this single experience helped me on my journey.

Practices

1) Find a trail with many branches—some shorter, others longer, some easier, others more difficult. Follow your heart. Let your heart determine your path. Quiet your mind. Try to enjoy. What, if anything, makes this difficult?

2) Undertake a project in the outdoors—planting a garden, raking the leaves, going on a hike or picnic, going cross-country skiing etc. How do you know when to stop? Do you stop? Why or why not? How important is the goal to you? How important is the process to you? How important is your heart? If others are with you, are you mindful of their presence and needs? Share.

3) Reflect on a time when you were faced with a difficult decision in the moment—one that you regret.

   a) How did you come to your decision? Was it an active or passive decision?
   b) Where were you on the Medicine Wheel? Do you understand how and why you made that decision?
   c) Now repeat Practice #3 using a decision that you can celebrate.

CHAPTER FIVE

Into the Darkness—The West Shield of Adolescence

Season—Fall
Element—Earth
Color—Black

Characteristics—adolescence, "I am", psyche, soul, introspection, insight, self-consciousness, hero's or heroine's journey, self-acceptance, initiation into change, shadow, self-esteem

Exaggerated Characteristics—addictions (the substance becomes "I am"), rebellion for the sake of rebellion, depression, helplessness, victim, self-inspection becomes self-indulgence, black and white thinking, self-loathing

And so we hold, and we let go, and pull, and lift, and ward—among rocks, around rocks, and over rocks. And now we go on through this solemn, mysterious way.

The river is very deep, the canyon very narrow . . . .
the waters reel and roll and boil, and we are scarcely
able to determine where to go.

John Wesley Powell

One thing that comes out in the myths is that at the
bottom of the abyss comes the voice of salvation. The
black moment is the moment when the real message of
transformation is going to come. At the darkest moment
comes the light.

Joseph Campbell in *The Power of Myth*

The West Shield

The diagram shows a circle divided into four shields with cardinal directions:

East Shield of Death and Rebirth (East)
Blue Road of Death
Letting Go
Transformation
Death, Release &

Characteristics:
transformation, birth,
death, rebirth, inspiration,
creativity, spirit, trickster
Exaggerated Characteristics:
visionary without embodiment,
dreams without action, everything
is love

North Shield of Adulthood (North)
Characteristics:
harmony, wisdom, rationality,
family, community,
action, bringing one's gifts
forward
"We Are"
Exaggerated Characteristics:
overly rational, linear, concrete
focus on mind without feelings

South Shield of Childhood (South)
Characteristics:
innocence, play, trust,
all senses, body, ego
"I"
Exaggerated Characteristics:
reactive, "I won't grow up!"
"I want it my way!"

West Shield of Adolescence (West)
Characteristics:
introspection, initiation
into change, shadow, self-
consciousness, hero's journey
"I am"
Exaggerated Characteristics:
rebellion, adddictions, depression,
self-loathing, victim, self-indulgent

LOST

I am little, perhaps four or five years old. My family is visiting neighbors at their recently purchased get-away cabin in the woods. I am familiar with woods because we often visit my aunt and uncle who are caretakers for a dairy farm. I love going to the woods. Wanting to get there makes the car ride long and boring. Once there, I am stuck listening to "grown-up" talk. I long for permission to go outside. Finally with admonitions and promises to stay within sight of the cabin, I am free. This is new territory, never before explored by me. I begin walking through the fall leaves which rustle and crackle underfoot. I am forever curious. There is that knife edge of excitement between adventure and danger. Periodically, I check to see that the cabin is in sight. I listen for sounds and am lost in the adventure. I turn around and the cabin has disappeared! Where did it go? It was right there! Where? At once I am filled with disbelief and terror. There is not only the terror of being lost, but also of getting in trouble for being lost! The latter is the more frightening, so I know I have to find my way back to the cabin. I try to remember the direction from which I have come. I make a guess but I am scared. I start walking in a direction, hoping to find the cabin. I am surprised that what first shows is a chimney, then a roof, and finally the sides of the cabin. Unknowingly, I have been walking down an incline, and being little, have lost sight of the cabin. I find my way "home", I learn an important lesson about terrain, and I never tell anyone about being lost.

Fast forward many years. I am backpacking in Wyoming's Wind River Range. Backcountry trails are usually well-defined. Still it is good to know how to use a compass and map. I am crossing a wash overgrown with willows and other foliage and I lose the trail. I move up and down, back and forth, trying to find the continuation of the trail across the wash—all to no avail. I remind myself that this is not a time to panic. I remember reading stories of others who have gotten lost, panicked, and died. Panic blocks your rational mind, and you make decisions contrary to those which would help you. Clear thinking is what is needed. I drop my pack and retrieve my compass. I use it to walk a bee-line, forty pace square to see if I can intersect the trail somewhere beyond the wash. I climb to higher ground and begin my pacing and intersect the trail. I retrieve my pack and move on. Found in the wilderness.

Reflections

There are many ways to lose one's path. And there are many ways to return to one's path. Whether in the natural world or on one's life journey, getting lost is disorienting. We seem to like to know where we are going. Fortunately or unfortunately, neither we nor the universe always cooperates in our desire to be in control of our destiny. Actually, life can be quite boring without the challenge of the unknown! The reality is that we all get lost on our life's journey around the Medicine Wheel. We get lost as we negotiate relationships, lost as we define our life's work, lost by our helplessness or our pride, lost by not admitting our not knowing, and lost by the challenges others put in our path. What defines us is what we do when we get lost. I learned early that I had to find my own way out of being lost. But that did not always serve me well. I had to learn to ask and receive help out of my lostness. And there were times when I wanted to be the victim, blamed others for my predicament, and hoped that someone would rescue me. These are just childlike and adolescent reactions to being lost, to feeling ungrounded and perhaps unsafe. All are part of the Medicine Wheel. Growing from childhood into adolescence and then into adulthood is not an easy process. It is fraught with the challenges of taking responsibility for one's actions, being clear about what one needs, and finding the appropriate resources to help. Sitting with the unknown, trusting the process, being deliberate, re-membering you are not alone, and "showing up" with intention are what we learn in the Shield of the West.

Practices

1) Find a nature center with trails that you can walk. Use the center's map to orient you as you explore. Begin to notice landmarks—a tree, a boulder, flowers, a bridge, for example—to augment the map. Determine the four directions. Use the map

and the sun/shadows to help. Then on future visits, travel without the map using it only as a check or if you become disoriented.

2) Learn how to use a map and compass. You can find resources at most outdoor stores.

3) A map and compass help to orient you in the natural world. What do you use as your map and compass in the human world?

   a) What are your tools?
   b) How easy is it to ask for help? Why or why not?
   c) Where do you go to develop new tools?

4) Map your life's journey, including the detours and explorations. If you got sidetracked or met detours, how did you re-orient yourself to your life path? What have you learned about yourself on your journey? What skills have you developed to help you find your way? What no longer serves you? In what way does your journey mirror the journey of others on the planet? How does it differ?

INTO THE DARKNESS AND THE UNKNOWN

A short backpacking trip in the Colorado Rockies has taken me up over the Continental Divide to the western slopes, and I am about to cross back over to the eastern slopes. With a sense of adventure, I decide that the next morning I want to be on top of the Divide to witness the sun rising in the east over the Great Plains. Camped well below tree line, I will have to get up in darkness to accomplish this goal. This will be an entirely new experience for me. I set the alarm on my watch for 4 a.m. and crawl into my sleeping bag for a short night. Never having considered anything like this before, I am filled with anticipation and sleep does not come easily.

The alarm wakens me. When I unzip my bag, cold air rushes in. "Do I really want to do this?" Determined, I dress in multiple layers, unzip the tent, peer out into darkness and am met by another blast of icy cold and a moonless sky filled with a thousand points of light. Hurriedly, I pack by the light of my flashlight which casts a small circle of luminescence as well as unwanted shadows. While focusing on packing, I am keenly aware of the looming darkness beyond the cast light. What lies beyond the light? What or who is watching me? I keep fear at bay with busyness. The nearby stream, whose many voices were welcome in the daylight, now carries the voices of unseen presences. Driven by the darkness and drawn by the sunrise, I cannot pack quickly enough. Finally I am packed and I hit the trail with flashlight in hand.

It is a short hike to the main trail, then a turn to the left, and a long, gentle uprise along one wall of a canyon which drops off to my right. My torch lights the trail immediately in front of me and I settle into a rhythm. The beam of my light dims and goes out, and I have no replacement batteries. Torchless, I am left to find the trail by starlight and night eyes. Occasionally the stillness is broken by the scurrying of unseen beings on the trail or in the underbrush. Though startled, I also find myself very curious about this night-time world—a world with which I am totally unfamiliar.

As the trail steadily rises toward the Continental Divide, the sky begins to lighten. Now above tree line, I sense a long, downward sloping tundra at the head of the canyon off to my right. Vague dark beings move over the tundra. Straining to see, to listen, to sense who or what travels with me, it is only with the growing light that I identify a small herd of elk. Then turning to look up the trail, I see the silhouette of a rack of antlers coming over the ridge. Stopping in my tracks, I watch the male of the herd top the ridge, walk down the trail towards me, and then move off into the tundra to be with his harem. Overwhelmed with pleasure and with an irrepressible smile, I hike on and gain the Divide.

With dawn's light, the beings of the night-time world disappear and those of the daylight arrive. The beat of a hawk's wings breaks the stillness. The Clark's Nutcracker calls and alerts to my presence. The stillness of the night air gives way to rushes of cold breeze. Finding the shelter of a few boulders against which to huddle, I watch the sun break over the Great Plains. The tundra comes alive with the orange light of the sun's rays, and I am warmed to the depth of my soul.

Reflections

For years I have focused on those few moments of sitting on top of the world watching the sunrise, listening to the sounds of the emerging day, feeling the warmth of the sun on my body, and savoring the cup of hot chocolate I had brewed on my small stove. In fact, that experience became my "safe place"—a place to which I can return in my mind's eye to calm myself and relax. In those years I was so focused on those moments that I completely lost the significance of what led to those few moments at the top of the world. I would not have had that experience without having traveled in the darkness. That night hike was an initiation. I met the darkness both within me and without. I met sounds and shadows from which I could no longer hide.

Every twenty-four hour period is a metaphor for life. We cannot live in the light alone—either the light of a twenty-four hour cycle or the light of our own being. In the natural world the Earth is the womb of all living beings. Darkness precedes light. Even the seed cannot grow until it reaches its tender shoots into the darkness of the earth. The seed is not afraid. It seeks the darkness so that it can be born into the light.

We, too, are of the earth. We, too, are creatures of the darkness and the light. If we do not acknowledge our own darkness—those thoughts, feelings, and acts we fear both in ourselves and in others—how can we know our light?

What do we fear in the unknown of the darkness? What creeps around out there and inside us that we do not want to meet? If we meet our own darkness and navigate the depths of that darkness, what will we discover about ourselves? About others? Are we willing to find the light in the darkness of our own being? And in the being of others?

What did I meet that night when I emerged from my tent, packed up, and hiked the trail? I met my fear of the unknown. I met the fear of being seen without seeing in return. I met my need to be in control. But I also found my courage to travel into the unknown with the knowing that the darkness would surrender to the light of day. As a child, I was terrified by the darkness. And on my first solo backpacking trip as an adult, I took a transistor radio with me to keep the sound of the night at bay. But on this night I began to "take back the night" both within and without.

In the years since, I have gone into the darkness many times—both nature's darkness and my own. Always I have found the gift of light at the end of the journey.

Practices

1) Find a place in the natural world where you can sit with the night—lean against a tree, sit in an open meadow, sit on a beach, sit on a rock, sit beside a stream. Let your eyes accommodate to the darkness, listen to the sounds, and let the darkness fill you.

   a) What do you experience? Whom do you meet? What do you hear? What feelings arise?

2) Go on a night walk on a moonless night. Let the darkness lead you.

   a) What does the darkness have to teach you on this night?
   b) Whom do you meet? Have a dialog with whomever you meet.
   c) Come home and journal about your experience.
   d) Is there some action you wish to take as a result of this experience? If so, plan how to accomplish that.

3) Go out in the early morning an hour before sunrise.

   a) What does the dawn have to teach you about the night?

b) Whom do you meet? Have a dialog with whomever you meet.

c) Come home and journal about your experience.

4) Make or obtain a noise maker—rattle, drum—something you can use with your hands. Take it with you on a night walk. As you walk, call in the spirits and send out healing to someone or to some being.

a) What happened?

b) What did you learn? Journal about your experience.

SPIDER

I am preparing to go on a Vision Quest. Four to six weeks before going, I am instructed to spend time in the wilderness looking for a sign—something that would make itself known to me. The meaning of its appearance I would take with me on my Vision Quest in Death Valley. I live in New Hampshire, so March means winter. Before dawn I am packed and in my car on the way north to the White Mountains. My intention is to cross country ski on the Wilderness Trail. As I arrive at the trailhead at sunrise, the air is cold and crisp. Once I begin skiing, the only sound is that of my skis cutting through icy snow. I am looking and listening for a sign and, of course, I am looking for something out of the ordinary. Despite my vigilance, nothing makes itself known.

At Franconia Brook, I cross the Pemigewasset River on snow-covered frozen bridges of ice so that I can ski down the other side of the river, thus making a loop. Never having crossed a river on snow bridges, I am nervous and hesitant. I am alone with no hope of another skier coming this way for a few hours. Is this smart? No, but I am not always smart or cautious. Gingerly I step out onto the snow and ice on my skis. I test the path ahead with my ski poles and inch forward. I look for the safest route or, at least, what I think is the safest route. I dread to hear the crack of breaking ice followed by my inelegant plunge into the river. The crack never comes. Very slowly I make my way to the far shore. I rest briefly and then continue my journey along the river back to the trailhead. Still there is no sign. Suddenly, I encounter a strong, musky odor and the wet tracks of an animal that has just come up from a watering place at the river's edge, crossed my trail, and disappeared into the woods. I am excited and hope for bear to be my sign, but I see nothing while exploring off trail. Disappointed, I return to the trail and ski on. Now I am nearing the end of the trail and still have found no sign. I am getting worried. What if I find no sign? Then suddenly my eyes catch something on the snow between my skis. I stop and study. It's a spider and it's alive! How can a spider be alive in twenty degree weather and on the snow? Immediately I state aloud, "Spider is not going to be my sign!" I do not like spiders. I dismiss the spider and look for another sign, returning home with a hemlock pine cone, the most common of cones in this forest!

In the next weeks, I find that I cannot escape spiders. They appear everywhere in my house. I meet a scientist whose specialty is spiders. Spiders are in books and on the television. All right! I surrender! Spider will be my sign! Now I have to make friends with spider. Obviously it has something to teach me. Spider goes with me on my Vision Quest.

Reflections

How often does the universe bring gifts to us and we turn away? And how many times must the gift be offered before we have the courage to accept the gift?

So often we are creatures of safety and status quo. We do not like to be knocked out of our comfort zone, and if we are knocked out of that zone we want to be in control of how, when, and where. Living with the known, uncomfortable as it may be at times, is preferred to the discomfort of the unknown.

Too many times I have ignored my intuition and listened to my ego to my detriment. I took a job even though I knew that half of the staff did not want to hire me. I collaborated with someone who needed to be in control. I put myself in relationship with someone who was a depressed alcoholic. All of these experiences caused me great pain. Each time I had a choice, I chose the very option that would put me in servitude and at risk.

What I have come to understand is, sooner or later, the darkness will overtake me. The darkness of the night is a metaphor for the darkness within me and the darkness within others. For years, I focused my anger on the darkness in others when I needed to be looking within and asking, "What is it about me that leads me to collude with the darkness of others? What do I need to shine a light on in my own being?"

I went out that morning trying to control what would make itself known to me. How often have I tried to control what happens? Yet the universe never tires of teaching me to surrender! Spider was a messenger. I took spider with me on my Vision Quest and she had much to teach me about the web of life, about her place in the mythology of the Native Americans, and about the spider in me. I thank spider for showing up and the universe for not letting me "off the hook."

Practices

1) Go out into the natural world and look for a sign. Allow it to make itself known to you. Now ask yourself, why has this shown itself at this time in my life? What is it here to teach me? After sitting with yourself and using your own inner knowing first, you may want to consult other resources to assist you. See Selected Bibliography.

2) Sit with yourself for the next half hour. Consider a decision you have recently made or are about to make. Answer these questions:

   a) What does my ego want?
   b) What does my intuition tell me is the best choice for me in this moment?
   c) To follow my intuition, what demons would I have to meet?
   d) What stops me from meeting them? What resources might be available to help me?

BEING IN SILENCE

Looking for a summer job, I use my teaching and
outdoor skills to land a job taking eleven junior high
school girls and boys along with a co-leader on a six-
week camping trip to the West. Our backpacks are
stuffed, and together with our tents and cooking gear,
are lashed to the top of the van. Packed and ready to go,
we leave New York City and head westward. Booked
into several national parks, I am looking forward to
specific opportunities including climbing Mt. Rainier.
After all, how difficult can it be to spend six weeks
with eleven young teens showing them the splendors
of the natural world?

Quickly, I discover just how much teens can talk.
Sardined in this van, the chatter is unceasing—
streams of talk of movies, music, boys, girls, and
anything else that keeps them from looking out the
windows at the passing landscape. Granted, some
of the landscape is repetitive and thus disinteresting
but, while I am looking out for wildlife, they are
busy getting to know the other ten teens squeezed
in with them. I learn that they and I come from very
different worlds. By twelve, I was already cooking
and doing family laundry (both of which I had to
teach to them on this trip) and the natural world
had become my constant companion, whereas it is
a foreign land to them. As for silence, I had learned
long ago that it was not only the safest strategy but
it brought rewards when in the natural world.

Having already stopped at Colorado's Rocky Mountain National Park, we are now in the Grand Tetons just finishing two days of rock climbing instruction and practice. Some, including me, have struggled through the second day as the climbing pitches became more difficult requiring more strength, height, and skill. There is an option on the third day to do a guided peak climb. Not everyone is interested, so we offer a day hike alternative that I am very willing to lead. Having hiked in the Tetons before, I know of a lovely hike that would bring us to an alpine lake.

Five teens sign up for the day hike. Everyone wants to see wildlife but, of course, we have been unsuccessful thus far because, even on the trails, talk is incessant. I am thinking about this as we drive to the trailhead. I want to see wildlife, too, but this will be a fruitless endeavor if this hike follows past form. Before setting out on the trail, I lecture, (yes, lecture) about the necessity of quiet if we hope to see any wildlife. Sensing this is an exercise in futility, we set off on the trail with a quiet pall hanging over our small band.

We enter a cool, dark forest. Sun seldom penetrates here because the forest canopy is so thick. Moisture is held here so the air is redolent of mud and decay. The forest closes in around us. Suddenly we hear the snapping of bushes on our left. We stop. The sounds build as some creature comes nearer. The air is filled with expectation—excitement fused with uncertainty. What can this be? We hold our collective breath as this creature approaches. Then out of the woods in front of us emerges a cow moose and newborn calf. The cow stops, takes the measure of us, then continues her way across the trail with her calf following on unsteady legs. Filled with awe and stunned into silence, there is no need now to remind anyone about walking and talking quietly. Everyone is smiling at one another in disbelief, and I am smiling and offering a silent "thank you" to spirit.

Now everyone is on alert for wildlife. Silently, we continue our hike but with a new focus. It is as if new eyes are seeing and new ears listening to what is around us. One of the girls sees a rabbit off the trail and mimes her excitement so that others will see, too. Now they listen and search for birds and watch the ever-present hawk circling overhead.

I begin to see fresh deer tracks leading up the trail ahead of us. My thought is that a doe is staying just ahead of us on the trail, and begin to wonder whether I can create another opportunity for wildlife meeting. Pointing out the tracks to my band, I suggest they wait here while I bushwhack up and around to be above the doe. Agreeing to my plan, I leave them and quietly walk, up through the sage, wildflowers, and trees until I am quite sure I am above the doe. Meeting the trail above, I begin a slow walk down to the teens. I never get to see the doe but my little band gets an up close and personal view. Again I thank spirit.

We arrive at an iced-in alpine lake but it is an anticlimax. It is the cake but we have already enjoyed the icing. That day something was learned about silence, about looking keenly, and listening for the silence between the sounds.

Reflections

How difficult it is to be alone with silence, alone with our own thoughts and feelings. The West Shield asks one to go inside to be introspective and self-conscious so that "I am" can emerge.

This is challenging in the adult world, too. How many of us bring our child-adolescent self with us to social situations. When we come together in groups we become talking animals. We find countless ways to claim "I" as we keep conversations going while making judgments about those with whom we are talking as well as judgments about ourselves. And how many of us abhor the silence? If we are not hooked into a computer, iPod, cell phone, or pager then the television is on, the music is playing, or talk radio is on. And if it is not sound that we use for distraction, it is the constant movement from one activity to another. We tend to be in constant states of stimulation and motion.

The transition from the "I" of childhood to the "I am" of the West Shield is a formative period of development. We can continue to age chronologically but remain in stages of childhood or adolescence, psychically and emotionally. This transition requires an emerging sense of self separate from the group. It is about not following others at a time when peer pressure is strong to be one of the crowd. The fear is being alone through rejection and judgment as the group exerts strong and unrelenting power. The tension of walking a line between belonging and building self-acceptance, self-esteem, and consciousness is palpable not only for young people but others of us still growing ourselves.

These young people were in unknown territory. They were strangers to each other, many came from privileged families in which they had few responsibilities, and none had experience living in nature. They were thrown back on what they knew—movies, music, and a need for hot showers and clean clothes. In many respects, the outdoors was a giant zoo. For some their knowledge was so minimal that the dangers of being in the natural world were unknown to them.

At the same time, these youngsters were missing meetings—meetings with the natural world, meetings with the self. When the group chatter ceased, they could meet the world with curiosity and awe. They found their eyes, they found silence, and the natural world unfolded. Suddenly they became partners with the world rather than boisterous spectators.

To be in the natural world, one must be willing to walk lightly, listen intently, speak in whispers, and see keenly. Let the world open to you. In this meeting we confront not only the other but also the self.

Practices

1) Go into the natural world and sit in silence for fifteen minutes, a half-hour, or an hour. Quiet the chatter in your mind. Listen. Look. Feel. What or whom do you meet? What tweaks your curiosity? What observations begin to coalesce? What are you learning about yourself? About others?

2) Repeat this experience in different seasons and in different weather.

3) Repeat this experience as a walking or moving meditation. Again, what or whom do you meet? What tweaks your curiosity? What feelings arise? What is the teaching?

4) Mark out a yard square piece of the natural world. Be with it for a half-hour. What do you notice? What do you learn?

5) When you are in social situations, who shows up—the "I," the "I am," or the "We?" Be curious about this. Is there a pattern? Is there a difference dependent upon the group? Who has the power over you—you, the group, a particular individual? Do you like who you are? If not, what might you work on in preparation for the next opportunity to be in a social situation? If you could repeat this situation, what would you do differently?

136 | Chapter Five

HUMBLED

Twice in the wilderness I thought I would not escape
with my life. When I was young, I had a sense of
immortality—an affliction of the young. I was reckless.
It took nature to teach me how puny I am.

It's the early 1970's and I am backpacking in Wyoming's
Wind River Range. The trails are rudimentary, no bridges
span watercourses, and there are no rules about where
to camp. On my second day I choose Barbara Lake,
because it carries my name, as my destination for that
night. The lake is above tree line and nestles in a bowl
surrounded by high peaks. Proud for having reached a
lake bearing my name, I make camp at the far end of the
lake, which allows for a view across the lake and down
a long valley. At dinner time, I am sitting in the opening
of my tent, eating my freeze-dried meal, and watching
clouds rolling up the valley towards me. The clouds close
in, thunder reverberates off the peaks, and the rains
come. It is not unusual to have a late afternoon storm
so I am more concerned about keeping bugs out of my
tent than a passing storm. Instead of passing, the storm
continues through the night, seemingly trapped within
the bowl of these 13,000 foot peaks. Rain drums against
my little tent. Lightning fills the sky almost without cease
and is followed by booming crashes of thunder. There
is but a second or two between flash and crash, and the
earth vibrates. Shaken by what is occurring out beyond
my tent, I worry about what will happen if lightning
strikes one of my tent poles as I lie in my sleeping bag

and on my sleeping pad. Having no control over what is happening all around me, I can only surrender and wait. Pulling my sleeping bag up over my head to block out the flashes of lightning, I plug my ears with my fingers and hope for sleep. Late at night the storms cease and I get two or three hours of sleep.

Dawn breaks to a gray, leaden sky. Relieved at having survived the night, I am about to find that the ordeal is not over. Sufficiently chastened for having chosen a campsite above tree line, I pack up my gear and head out on the trail. Almost immediately, I pass the bleached bones of a large animal whose mortal life ended in this place some time ago. The ground underfoot is sodden. What were rills of water yesterday are now fast-moving streams. And streams are now swollen torrents. High mountain meadows have not just one watercourse flowing through them but several, each of which must be crossed. Overwhelmed and not thinking clearly, I see no way across these streams except to jump. Of course, I fall in, scramble up the far bank, and change into dry clothes. My next strategy is to ford, so I take off my boots and socks, roll up my pants, use a stick for added balance, and successfully cross. This becomes usual. Some places, however, look too dangerous to ford so I climb upward along water falls to find safer crossings. To say I am scared is an understatement. I am not worried about drowning as much as I am worried about falling and becoming injured in such a way that I cannot continue. I am witness to the power of nature and shrunken to the measure of my humanness in the natural world.

A second encounter with the power of nature occurs on a guided climb on Colorado's Longs Peak. We are planning to chimney up to a narrow ledge named Broadway and then to continue our climb up the left side of the Diamond Face to the summit. Because thunder storms are common in the eastern slopes of the Rockies, we have set out at 4 a.m. to get to the climbing site by 7 a.m. and plan to climb, summit, and be off the summit by early afternoon.

There are three of us plus our guide and we are all carrying climbing gear—ropes, carabiners, crampons, and ice axes. I have climbed here before but this route requires chimneying which is new to me. It is cold and wet inside the chimney but we all top out onto Broadway. Broadway is a misnomer. It is a ledge which is at most two feet wide that runs below the Diamond Face. From Broadway, there is a 2000-foot drop down to Chasm Lake and 2000 feet up to the summit. Having reached Broadway, we are ready for the next leg of the climb. It is still early morning and we note an unusual storm building in the east and heading west toward us. This means we will be exposed to lightning strikes on the East Face of the mountain if the storm hits. There is no option except to abort the climb if we wish to remain safe.

We begin our retreat by hiking south on Broadway to reach the top of the Lamb Slide. This is an 800-foot trough of snow, ice, and rocks which descends to a boulder field. Roped together, shod with crampons, and ice axes in hand, we begin our descent, which has a significant pitch. Most of us are novices and are unsure about walking down this pitch. One or another of us tries to control the fear of falling forward by leaning too far backwards. I fall and reach the end of my tether, stand up, and continue walking. Someone else falls and the process is repeated. From afar this must look like something out of the Keystone Cops but for us, the storm is building and we have to get off the mountain so, from our point of view, this is not funny.

Our guide, responsible for our safety and worried about the slowness of our descent, suggests we hurry the process of escape by lying face down on the snow, head uphill, ice axe in ready position for a controlled descent and allow ourselves to slide downhill. He tells us he will set up an ice axe belay so as to play out our climbing rope slowly thus helping to control our descent. When the rope is played out, we will stop, stand up, and await his joining us and setting a new belay. As low person on the rope, thus closest to the boulder field below, I am skeptical about this plan but, having nothing to offer other than my anxiety, I say nothing. We begin our descent sliding ever downward on our stomachs. While descending I am also intensely aware of the moment. The ride is not smooth but bumpy as my body runs over imbedded rocks. Snow finds its way under my jacket and shirt and I am getting wet. Soon we are jerked to a stop when our rope is played out. We stand and await our guide. He arrives, sets a new belay, and we begin our second descent. The slide down seems longer this time, and I dare to look up, only to see all of us, guide included, in a free fall. We are all falling toward the boulder field and sure injury, if not death. Desperately I use my ice axe and crampons and succeed in stopping myself. The climber above me, who is without an ice axe, rolls over me and pulls me free of the mountain. There is no stopping gravity's pull, just an unrelenting battle to stop before we crash into the boulders! Each of us is lost in his or her personal struggle to survive, yet we are all tethered together. We stop. As lowest person on the tether, I am fifteen feet from the boulder field. Physically trembling, I inch my way to the boulders. What was the source of my fear in the free fall now becomes my touchstone for safety. So very grateful to be sitting on a boulder, I try to collect myself and calm my nerves. We are all thankful that not one of us gave up but fought to the very last. It is a quiet group. There is no bravado. We appreciate how fortunate we are to be alive and uninjured. It begins to rain. Still, we do not move. It is storming up on the mountain. Suddenly there is a loud rumble. Looking up to Broadway, a thousand feet above us, we watch a huge rock slab peel off and plunge to the rock debris below. Looking for falling bodies, I see none. Is this where we stood on Broadway earlier in the morning? Silently we collect our gear and begin our long trek out to the trailhead. Nature has spared us and we have spared ourselves to live another day.

Reflections

What do you do when your life is on the line? Even more fundamental, why put yourself in such situations? Is my life always on the line?

Here in the first story, I am foolish. With reckless denial of my mortality, I put myself in imminent danger by camping above tree line simply because I wanted to stay at a lake that carried my name. Clearly I was not educated about weather above treeline. I was terrified through the night. And my fear carried into the next day when I found every place flooded. In the early morning I was not thinking clearly or logically. How could I have possibly jumped over a rushing stream with a fifty pound pack on my back? Of course I would fall in. As the day progressed, my rational mind took over and I made more deliberate decisions as I negotiated various obstacles. Learning an important lesson about treeline and thunderstorms, I was shrunk down to my size—small human body cocooned in a sleeping bag inside a tiny tent surrounded by 13,000 foot peaks and nature's fury. I never did that again!

In the latter story, storms from the east are a rarity in the Rocky Mountains. On the eastern slopes, one can predict a summer thunderstorm from the west sometime in the afternoon. This is why hikers and climbers try to summit before noon and then begin their descent. Here a combination of factors—deteriorating weather, level of skill, and the popping out of a belay contributed to our free fall. Here fear of crashing on the boulders below became a motivator. Tethered together, we were a team and no one surrendered to gravity's inevitability. Thus, together we were spared. Weather is always a factor and, obviously, is unpredictable. Preparation, necessary equipment, skills, knowledge, and a will to live help us to survive.

As a culture the idea of man or woman against nature is core to the ethic that settled this land. Manifest Destiny called our ancestors westward. That quest was romanticized into the hero's or heroine's journey in books, movies, and television. These were the stories with which I grew up. Stories of conquering nature and those in the way of white man's desire to settle and tame the land.

Industrialization followed the settling of the West. We took bigger steps in harnessing nature and making it subservient to our desires. We moved the mountains, dammed the rivers, denuded the landscape, harvested the forests, and polluted the water and air. We think we can conquer nature. Yet yearly, nature reminds us of its power—the floods, hurricanes, earthquakes, tsunamis, blizzards, and volcanic eruptions. All are reminders that in the face of nature's power we are puny beings. When we live in the West Shield of the Medicine Wheel, we try not to know that. Instead we try to claim our superiority—we attack the mountain when we hike, we leave rain gear and warm clothing at home along with our compass, a map, flashlight, extra food, and water. We are prideful and foolish. We ignore the weather. We are lucky if we escape with our lives intact. An encounter with the power of nature reminds us of our place and prepares us for living both in and with nature. It prepares us for finding a new and more mature relationship with the self and the world.

Practices

1) All of us have had to learn to live with nature in one way or another—learning to carry an umbrella, carrying survival gear in our car during the winter, living through an extended power outage, etc. And if you have spent any time in the natural world, you have also had to confront nature in its rawest forms.

   a) Reflect back on one or more of these meetings. How did you react to the discomfort? Where would you place yourself on the Medicine Wheel during this experience?
   b) What did you learn about yourself? About others?
   c) If you could have done it differently, what would you have had to change about you? How might you do that?

2) Industrial civilization continues to invade the natural world. We settle in flood plains, build on earthquake faults, live where water is a scarce commodity, build in fire-prone canyons and on avalanche-prone mountainsides. We are scared

and angry when mountain lions or other wild denizens "invade" our territory. We willingly risk our lives and those of our loved ones.

a) How willing are you to live with nature and not against it?
b) How willing are you to accept nature's terms?
c) How willing are you to share precious resources with your neighbors?
d) Are you willing to give up your green lawn? Your flower gardens? Your golf courses? Your spectacular view? Your long commute? Your life?
e) If not, what is your plan for the next cataclysm?
f) If yes, what plans have you made to survive? To die? To lose all you own? To share the burden with your neighbors?

3) Go for a journey in the natural world. How will you prepare yourself? What will you take with you? What will you do if the weather suddenly changes? How prepared are you if you become injured, disoriented or lost?

BEAR AND RATTLESNAKE

In thirty-five years of backpacking, I had never met a bear or a rattlesnake. Mostly I have avoided areas where grizzly bears live, but most other places I have hiked and backpacked have resident bears. And though I have chosen not to hike in the southeastern states, venomous snakes do live in most areas that I have explored.

Two days from completing a forty-five-mile circle route in the King's Canyon area of California, I meet a father and son packing into the wilderness. We stop to exchange bits of information about what lies ahead of each of us. They tell me that a large brown bear visited their campsite around six the previous evening.

My fears about bears are two-fold: I do not want to meet a sow and her cub for I know the sow will be very protective, will act from instinct, and will not know that I mean no harm; and I do not want a curious and hungry bear to invade my food stores. Here in King's Canyon, backcountry sites are furnished with bear boxes, metal containers anchored to the ground and doors secured with snap link hooks and chains. In other backcountry areas, I have to bear-bag all food, soaps, and toothpaste, and suspend the bags with rope from the branch of a tree. Hopefully the bags are high enough from the ground and far enough from the tree trunk to discourage any hungry bear. Twice I have met backcountry parties aborting their planned trip after a bear had invaded their stores. Once a bear has gotten the taste of food or toothpaste, it is difficult to drive it away from the site. To me, a bear foaming at the mouth with toothpaste or soap would be quite a sight, if it would only leave my food!

It is midday when I arrive at the campsite that the father and son stayed at the previous night. After setting up camp, there is ample time to clean up, relax, explore, and write before dinner. Deciding to outfox the bear, I plan to eat at five. At the appointed time, I retrieve my freeze-dried food from the bear box, then turn to see a large brown bear walking towards my site. So much for fooling the bear! Quickly I return the food to the bear box and go to retrieve my camera from my tent. This deserves a picture! The bear is about thirty feet away when it turns and begins to circle my site. This is fine with me for I am taken by the excitement and pleasure of meeting a bear in the wilderness. But then the bear turns and begins to walk towards me. Oh my! This is not OK! What am I to do now? Back in the northeast, I have been able to scare off bears by yelling. Maybe that could work here? Raising my arms over my head, I find my voice and begin yelling. To my utter astonishment, the bear turns and runs uphill away from my site. "Yes, I am woman!" I exclaim. Such power claimed! Retrieving my dinner contents from the bear box, I enjoy my meal while sitting at a small campfire, but I keep looking over my shoulder to see if the bear is returning. Once I see it walking along the trail above my campsite, but it does not venture down to me. In the morning before arising, I can hear it sniffing around my tent, but I know I am safe, for all my food and other items of interest are safely closed in the bear box. I have met bear.

Now I am on the trail heading back to the trailhead I had left seven days ago. I am perhaps a half hour from my campsite, hiking through an area of a recent forest fire and already thinking about the "real" dinner I will enjoy tonight when, without warning, there is a rustling noise in the new undergrowth just to my left. A rattlesnake slithers its way across the trail and stops on a small ledge to my right. Knocked out of my reverie and brought back to the present moment, I stop. Here is the very thing I most fear meeting. Yet instead of fear, there is wonder. We eye each other from this distance of eight feet. I talk to it. It lies still and stretched out. What do I see? I see a creature shorter and slimmer than I had created in my fearful mind's eye. Counting the rattles, I realize it is only six or seven years old. Asking aloud how it had escaped the fire, I honor its hard existence. We are at peace in meeting each other. Finally I move on, but not without respect and admiration for the rattlesnake and for myself. I am just a woman meeting my fear, my demon and finding myself honoring its presence in my life!

Reflections

For years I was stuck between the South and West Shields whenever I feared encountering poisonous snakes, especially rattlesnakes. Any snake causes me to jump and I give them all a wide berth. Deliberately I have put myself in environments friendly to rattlesnakes. Knowingly doing that has ended up paralyzing me with fear. But clearly, like the moth drawn to the flame, I have had unfinished business with rattlesnakes. I am more comfortable with bears. Having met them in my yard when they come to raid my bird feeders, I have learned that they run when I make a lot of noise. Now I know that rattlesnakes are not out to "get me" nor I them. I know when they are curled, startled, or trapped, they will strike out of self-protection. I will still be vigilant, after all, I am invading their territory. In all likelihood, I will still jump. But now I have met Bear and Rattlesnake. I respect each and honor their place in the wilderness. Meeting Bear and Rattlesnake reminds me that what one knows through reading is not fully known until one experiences it, takes it in at a deep cellular level, and makes it one's own.

This is a story of coming full circle. It is a story about the death of a part of me that had always kept me being an outsider in the wilderness. Until I could meet bear and rattlesnake with equanimity, I could not truly be part of the wilderness in which I was living. To date, it was my last backpacking trip. Bear, rattlesnake and I—we were each seen, we met with respect and honor. As a result, I was free to take on new challenges. In coming full circle on the Medicine Wheel, I am free to begin a new circle. Where will this new circle lead?

Practices

1) Go find something in the natural world with which you are not comfortable. Start small. For example, let an ant or spider or worm crawl on your hand or up your arm. Meet it. Be with it. Watch it. Thank it for its presence. Study it—its color, its texture. Feel its travel. What is its place in the web of life? What does it teach you about you? What does it teach you about courage? What is its path around the Medicine Wheel? In relation to this being, where are you on your path around the Medicine Wheel?

2) Reflect on your own life. Think about the fears you have met and come full circle. Be specific. Honor these places of growth. What qualities did you rely upon or develop that allowed you to meet these fears?

3) Now think about those places where your fears keep you stuck. What are your fears? List them. Focus on one of them. What do you already know about yourself that may help you to meet this fear? Are there external resources that could help you meet this fear? If this fear did not hold you back, what would you be free to do? Now what do you need to do to grow more fully into your being?

FEAR AND LOATHING

For years I allowed fears to govern my life—fear of monsters, failure, not being good enough, being shamed, and being seen among them. I felt little, vulnerable, and always at risk of being "found out." I hated my fear and I hated myself. No one noticed, at least no one who dared speak of it.

I used my fear to motivate me. To the outside I may have appeared successful, but on the inside the dark grip of fear held me captive. Always I was driven to stay one step ahead of anyone finding out that I was empty and terrified.

Thankfully, as a young child I had several pleasurable experiences in the natural world and I found nature to be a place of safety from the challenges of the human world. During later adolescence I focused on finding my place in an adult world and lost the safety of the natural world. Fear continued to be a constant companion despite my efforts and my successes. In my early 20's I found my way back to nature through the gifts of geography and the happenstance of summer jobs. Of course I brought my fears with me. Though I hated my fears, I used them sometimes to motivate me, hoping I would eventually outdistance one or more.

- A small group of senior girl campers, a co-leader, and I are on a three-day traverse of the Presidential Range in New Hampshire's White Mountains. We have prepared for this trip by completing a series of increasingly difficult hikes. This is the first time the girls are not hiking with the boys from the brother camp. In past years the boys often carried their and the girls' gear when the girls tired! I am determined to prove our ability to do this without the boys.

On the first day we hike up to the hut on Mount Madison. The next day dawns raw and wet. A ranger checks our gear and clears us to traverse the range to Lake of the Clouds Hut on Mount Washington. He suggests that we start out before he leaves so we will be ahead of him on the trail; thus he could catch up with us should we run into difficulty. This is my first experience in leading an overnight trip in the White Mountains and the weather worries me; but the ranger's support reassures me.

We set out in a heavy mist. We are in the clouds. When we leave the protection of the mountain bowl, we are blasted by rain and a cold wind that rips at our rain gear. We stop to tie down ponchos and gear. The wind is cold and increasing. Enclosed in the clouds, we hike through a surreal landscape of grotesque formations that alternately appear and disappear in the swirls of mist.

Preoccupied by these ephemeral monsters and the thought that we are in dangerous conditions, I mindlessly step onto a boulder, transfer my weight, and my right foot slips forward colliding with another boulder. I am wearing sneakers (this is long before hiking boots) and feel a sharp pain in my big toe. Certain that it is broken, I do not want to alarm anyone, so we hike on. Now my concerns are not only how to get across the range safely, but also how to minimize the pain in my big toe. The traverse is a seven-mile hike mostly above tree line. We follow the trail by looking for rock cairns or paint marks on rocks. In some places, due to the density of the clouds, we proceed one cairn at a time. Worrying someone will become separated from the group, the co-leader, looking as concerned as I, follows up the rear to herd everyone in front of her. The combination of wind, temperature, and wet clothing make hypothermia a definite possibility, so we cannot afford to take time to rest, snack, or drink water. Quickly, this turns into a forced march. Silently, I carry three thoughts with me—press on, step gingerly, and the ranger is behind us. Other than that, I am totally focused on getting us across the range safely. Without rest or detour to the summit of Mount Washington, we arrive at the hut long before anyone expects us. We are soaked through and through, chilled to the bone, but safe. The hut becomes a dry, warm, and welcome shelter. The ranger never comes.

Anxieties and fears accompany me on every trek into the mountains. What must I do to return safely to the trailhead? What must I carry with me? What decisions must I make to keep me safe? Regardless of my preparation and efforts, there will always be the unknown that I am fated to meet—a trail to find; a river to ford; a thunderstorm above tree line; the pounding of a hail storm; a summer snowstorm that collapses my tent; a rockslide; physical exhaustion; or tripping and falling.

- I am on a solo backpacking trip along the Merced River in Yosemite National Park. My plan is to hike up to the river's source. In four days I reach the high meadows and then run into last winter's snow. How far dare I venture? Totally alone up here and fearful of falling through snow undercut by melt, I retreat to the high meadows and base camp there for an extra day. Then I begin to return via the trail I followed on the way into this wilderness. Three days from the trailhead, I am crossing a small water source on a log. With a loud crack, the log gives way. Falling, I reach out to catch myself. My right hand collides with wood followed by a sharp pain and I know instantly that I have broken a bone in my right hand or wrist. My first thought is, "I'm glad it was not my ankle." But now what do I do? Focus becomes critical. I remind myself, "Stay clear-headed. Do not panic. Work this out." Worried about taking my pack off and then trying to hoist it back on again, I dismiss the idea of making a sling with a bandanna stuffed somewhere in my pack. Remembering that I am a few miles from a backcountry ranger station, I decide to head for there to get help with a sling. I hope someone will be there.

Holding my right hand up into the air to limit swelling, I hike slowly and deliberately. I reach the station, call out and, gratefully, someone responds. Explaining my predicament, I ask the ranger to retrieve a bandana from my backpack. She fashions a sling to hang onto my pack. Now my right hand can rest in this sling. Assuring the ranger that I will be alright and explaining my exit plans, I thank her for her help and continue on to a backcountry campsite.

Now my thoughts turn to the challenges of setting up my tent, preparing dinner, eating, and organizing for the night with only my non-dominant hand and the leverage of my two lower extremities. Arriving at the camping area, I select a likely spot away from other backpackers and begin this new adventure. Some tasks are easy but others much more challenging. There is just no way to strike a match and light a stove without two hands! Obviously, the pain has to be endured. And as careful as I try to be, my right wrist gets jostled or knocked, the pain peaks and then becomes a dull throb. By dusk I am ready for sleep so take pain pills, crawl into my sleeping bag, gingerly try to zip it up, and hope that I will not have to get up in the middle of the night to pee. Sleep is fitful. The next morning there is the breaking of camp. Never having stuffed a sleeping bag with one hand and two feet before, I struggle and fight sack and bag, and finally have to fudge using my right hand a little. My hand hurts but I do not want to take too many pain killers for I have a full day of hiking and another night on the trail before I reach civilization. Despite efforts to keep my hand elevated, the swelling has increased. Any fears or thoughts about not reaching the trailhead safely are pushed aside. Instead I am focused on the challenge of getting there by relying on my own problem-solving and physical skills. One change I must make is to alter my take-out plan which was to hike back up to my car. Instead I will hike directly down into Yosemite Valley on the third day so I can go directly to the Valley Hospital for X-rays and a splint prior to taking a local bus back to my car.

Reflections

In Soulcraft[4], Bill Plotkin shares a beautiful story about the butterfly, a wonderful creature of transformation, and its companion, the caterpillar. He tells us to look closely at the sides of a caterpillar to find the small dots of color strategically placed down the sides of its body. It has come to be known scientifically that

---

4   Bill Plotkin, *Soulcraft: Crossing Into the Mysteries of Nature and Psyche* (Novata, CA: New World Library, 2003), pp 77-78.

the caterpillar experiences these dots as foreign to its being as a caterpillar. It cannot dispose of the spots so must endure them. Soon, by nature, the caterpillar is compelled to spin its cocoon. Once spun and enclosed, the caterpillar dissolves into an ooze. Now those little spots come into play. These spots carry what is necessary for the brown ooze to be transformed into the butterfly. Without those little colorful dots, there would be no butterfly and there would be no caterpillar!

How many times do we attempt to hide or reject aspects or qualities of the self that we have grown to dislike or have been ridiculed or rejected by others? In a society focused on health, beauty, and the young, how many of us work hard to be a particular size or physically fit? How many of us hide our age? Or how many of us have heard, "Oh, don't be so sensitive" as if sensitivity is a trait the world does not need? How many have tried to hide their heredity to "pass" or their gender preference in order to be safe and accepted? And how many other things do we try to hide from ourselves or others—a history of mental illness, family history, or disabilities? All in all, we are rather judgmental of others as well as of ourselves. Of course we would be judgmental of others if we could not be accepting of who we are. To accomplish this, each of us has to be willing to be her or himself fully and embrace all that she or he is. That means being willing to enter the darkness of the West Shield. When one is afraid to meet the self fully then one is afraid to meet the other as well.

Just as the caterpillar dislikes those dots, I have hated my fear. I have been on a journey to find *common ground* with my fear. I have been perched at the precipice of an abyss. Do I run back from the abyss or do I step forward into the unknown? Sometimes I run and sometimes I move forward. But seldom did I really allow myself to embrace the fear or give voice to the fear. Often I relentlessly drove myself forward and, fortunately, the universe has been kind to me, for I am still here in this body and in this time and place. In that process, the natural world has revealed to me its beauty and its ugliness, its serenity, and its raw power. It has mirrored back to me my beauty and my ugliness, my serenity and my power. I can choose not to be driven by fear. I can choose to neither run nor jump. I can simply choose to meet my essence, all that is me, without judgment. I can simply choose my humanity rather than choosing to hate or to love my fear. Like the caterpillar and the butterfly, I can allow myself to transform. I am.

Practices

1) Arrange a costume party for 8-10 adults. Each person is to be an archetypal person, famous person, or an animal, and to dress accordingly. Each person is to take on the persona of that being in his/her interactions with all the other beings in the next hour or so. Pay attention to your reactions to yourself and to the others. To

whom are you drawn? Whom do you avoid? Why? What are others' reactions to you? How do you feel about yourself? Do others' reactions influence how you feel about yourself? After the party, come together to share experiences and feelings. What did you learn about your fear and loathing?

2) Think of someone with whom you interact but would just as soon avoid. What bothers you about this person? Why does it bother you? What are your feelings about this person? Does this person remind you of someone in your past? If so, who? Rather than avoiding, what one small step can you take for yourself that might help you to become unstuck? How might you find *common ground* with this person?

3) Group task: Create a simple task that has to be accomplished by the group, for example setting up a schedule for the use of a facility. Divide the group into two groups based on a physical characteristic— height, eye color, hair color, etc. Label one group as the group favored by society and the other group as the less favored. Work to complete the task with people in each group playing out their assigned positions in society. Pay attention to what happens to each of you. What happens in the group as the task is engaged? What are your feelings? What surprises you about you? What is there for you

to learn from this experience? What lies beneath loathing? Share in the large group.

4) Is there some quality about yourself that you loathe? Name it. Do you run from it? Do you cover it up? Do you use it to motivate yourself? Can you welcome it into your being? How might you do that? Journal.

CHAPTER SIX

Bearing Gifts and Building Community—
The North Shield of Adulthood

Season—Winter

Element—Air

Color—White

*Characteristics—adulthood to elderhood, "we are,"
rational mind, wisdom, community, family, other
love, action, claiming one's gifts, sharing one's gifts,
harmony, appreciation*

*Exaggerated Characteristics—overly rational, mind-
oriented, workaholic, linear, concrete, rigid, devoid
of feeling, form is valued rather than spirit*

Snowflakes are one of nature's most fragile things, but
just look what they can do when they stick together.

Vesta M. Kelly

One of the signs of passing youth is the birth of a sense of fellowship with other human beings as we take our place among them.

Virginia Wolff

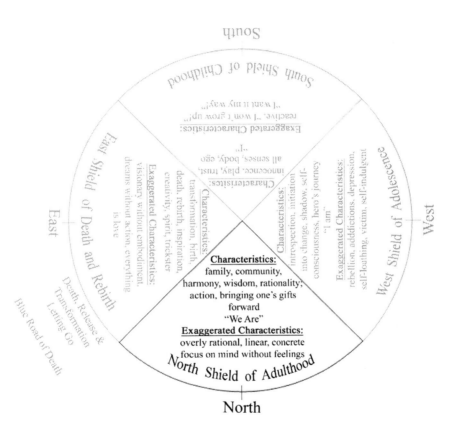

The North Shield

LESSONS IN COMMUNITY

Redwoods are the majestically tall trees growing along the Pacific coast from south of Monterey, California to southern Oregon. The long, slender trunks and canopy reach heights of 300-350 feet. The redwoods are heavily dependent upon water to survive. They grow in areas where the canopy, an ecosystem unto itself, can be bathed in ocean fogs and the roots can drink up the coastal rains. Pacific storms often crash into the coast driven by powerful winds. Despite their height and top heavy canopy, the redwoods have a shallow root system extending outward in a concentric circle from the trunk. So how can trees reaching 300 feet into the sky, with a top-heavy canopy and a shallow root system, survive the coastal winds? Each redwood intertwines its roots with the roots of the redwoods in its immediate area. Thus there is an underground mat of intertwined roots creating a family or community of trees.

On the eastern side of California, sagebrush bushes live in the high desert of Death Valley. If you were to stand on a desert hill and look out over the landscape, you would see these bushes spaced far apart as if planted by a desert gardener knowing each needs space in which to survive. Here water is a precious and scarce resource. Though the sagebrush may be only four or five feet high and equal in circumference, its roots reach out in a twenty-foot wide concentric circle. In this way the sagebrush can maximize its uptake of water from the infrequent storms.

Reflections

In order to survive, the redwood and the sagebrush have uniquely adapted to their respective environments. The redwood ensures its survival by creating a close-knit community in which the survival of one means the survival of all; whereas the sagebrush, in order to ensure its survival, maintains distance and clear boundaries between itself and others of its species. Are we any different as human beings?

Oftentimes we approach life as one person against the world. In our quest for upward mobility, our focus on our own individual success comes at the expense of others. It is often how leaders see their country vis-à-vis the rest of the world. Whether individually, in groups, in states, or in countries, we tend to focus on our own needs without regard to those of others. In fact, our approach can often be one of "I" versus "It" in which the other is objectified. This is a marker of being in the South Shield. When there is a disaster or a crisis that touches our lives, we seem to remember our common humanity and reach out to one another. Here the North Shield awakens us to our *common ground*. A human crisis or disaster renews our consciousness and reminds us that we are, indeed, connected to one another. Why? Why do we need a disaster or threat to be able to treat one another as "Thou" rather than "It"? Why do we need a common enemy—another country, a religion, or nature—before we can find our common humanity?

I remember the northeast blackout in the 1960's when the area was plunged into darkness—elevators stopped between floors, trains stopped in tunnels— all the machinery and appliances dependent upon electricity simply stopped. During this time people came together to support and aid one another, and the incidence of crime in cities actually went down. There have been natural and manmade disasters since then and we find that we have a great capacity for empathy, support, and connection. In this way, we are like the redwoods in that we find strength in our reaching out—giving and receiving.

On the other hand, as with the sagebrush, we need clear boundaries so that we have a clear sense of self and other. How does one make connection with others without putting oneself in servitude to the other? Certainly on a day-to-day basis we can share our gifts, both material and immaterial, but to maintain both service to self and other, we must know how to shepherd our resources so as to be replenished and not depleted. For example, we can share our material resources—money and goods—but must be careful to not put ourselves at risk. It is in time, services, and energy that we must be even more judicious. It is all too easy to share these aspects of ourselves without thought to our own needs and then find ourselves depleted and burned out. This is a constant concern with those working in helping professions, parents in families, and others reaching out around the world. We ask much of those who give of themselves. When exhaustion or burnout arrives, it becomes more difficult not only to honor the other as "Thou" but also to honor the self as "Thou." Knowing how to share our gifts without putting ourselves in servitude is the wisdom of the North Shield.

Practices

The redwood survives by intertwining its roots with those of other redwoods while the sagebrush needs space in order to survive.

1) Think about yourself as a tree. How deeply do your roots run? Whom does your canopy touch? Who reaches towards you? What other trees live around you—size, age, type? To whom do you provide sustenance? Are you satisfied with who you are and your place in the community of living things?

2) When darkness and chaos comes into your life, are you like the redwood or sagebrush? In what ways? Are you satisfied with your place in the community of human beings?

3) If you are like the redwood, does the sagebrush have a lesson for you?

4) If you are like the sagebrush, does the redwood have a lesson for you?

5) What do you do to balance self and community? Are there changes you wish to make in that balance? If so, what?

6) An ecosystem is a larger community of beings. Go out into an aspect of the natural world, for example a woods, a pond, a desert, a tidal zone. Consider how the beings in this ecosystem co-exist. What do you do to live together in your human community? What is it that you contribute?

UP CLOSE AND PERSONAL

The strident calls of blue jays fill the air most of the year. Yet in nesting time, they become quiet as church mice. It is late spring and suddenly there are loud raucous alarm calls of the blue jays, and I am alerted as are all the other creatures in the area. Without seeing, I know what is taking place. A hawk or crow has invaded the territory looking for a young nestling to snatch up and carry off. Having been witness to this before and philosophical about the circle of life, I catch sight of a small hawk emerging from the woods and pursued by angry, boisterous blue jays. Just a bystander, I have removed myself from this struggle for survival.

Now I am driving to work in the early morning. There is a big, dark lump in the middle of the westbound lane and I slow down to look. There are no oncoming cars so, pulling into the eastbound lane, I see the lump is a snapping turtle making its way across the road to lay its eggs. She has pulled herself into her shell as traffic speeds by. This is a heavily traveled road and I am moved to undertake a rescue by helping her across the road. Stopping my work-bound travel, I pull over, hop out, pop the car trunk, and retrieve a plastic scoop. Past experience reminds me that coaxing this turtle across the road will not work, so my plan is to scoop her up and carry her across the road. The turtle's head emerges from the shell and she eyes me warily. Knowing enough to approach from the rear, I wave westbound traffic into the oncoming lane so that together, the turtle and I can execute this plan. As I near, the turtle rises up on her front legs, spins to face me, and hisses a warning. Stunned by her speed, I try again to maneuver myself behind her, again she spins, and this time the head darts out and jaws snap shut with such ferocity that the audible snap makes me shudder. Her ferocity scares me. Fear rises up from the pit of my stomach. Simultaneously I am watching for traffic and watching the turtle. The turtle and I are doing a circle dance in the middle of the highway! Each time I try to scoop her up, she spins and snaps. We are locked in a battle of survival. Eye to eye with the rawness of nature, I lunge forward and scoop before she can fully spin, and succeed in flipping her onto her back. Moving in before she can right herself, I scoop and lift landing her upright in the earth beside the road. She eyes me; she does not move nor does she hide in her shell. Having accomplished what I set out to do, I humbly retreat to my car. I am shaking. Glimpsing into the rear view mirror, I see she still watches me. Her animal ferocity, her will to live remains with me for a very long time.

Reflections

I know my intent in this encounter. I see what I am about to do as an act of compassion and community as I understand it. But the turtle only knows about survival. She sees me as a predator. Though I mean her no harm, she only knows what she must do to survive. I am at once admiring of her will to survive and terrified by her ferocity. I wonder how many times she has crossed this man-made invasion of her territory. Her shell back to front measures about 16 inches or so, and I imagine there have been many years of road crossing. Hopefully others have helped her on her journey. At the same time I sense how easily I could lose a finger or two to those snapping jaws. Yet I am driven by not wanting to see a turtle carcass smashed on the road.

Later I begin to think more deeply about my act. Should I have acted to rescue this single creature? Should I have let "nature" take its course? Are our technology, our roads, and our vehicles part of the circle of life? Am I a member of the circle or an intruder? When am I member? When am I an intruder? When am I merely a witness? With the hawk and the jays, I stood on the outside of the circle and let "nature" take its course. What was different for me in these two situations?

Several years ago, one dark summer night in New York City, a young woman was attacked on the street and murdered. Many people in their apartments heard her screams and cries for help. No one came. No one called the police. Everyone remained shuttered in their apartments while a young woman died alone. When we close ourselves off from one another and from all creatures, don't we diminish ourselves while we are busy turning other beings into "other"? If we risk meeting and knowing each other, might we come to honor and love all that is here? Everything here is sacred.

The sustainability of my life, of all lives is intimately interwoven with the sustainability of all beings.

Practices

1) Where was the act of rescuing the turtle on the Medicine Wheel? Was I in the North Shield or the South Shield? Why? Where was I on the Medicine Wheel with regard to the hawk and jays? Why?

2) What would you have done if you had met turtle? Why?

3) What life have you spared today? What life have you taken?

4) Some say that when a butterfly moves its wings in China, the breeze is felt in North America. What do you think?

5) Have there been times in the human world when you have wanted to protect or help another? What did you do? Why? What does it require of you to act?

6) Reflect on a time you walked away from your own moral and spiritual compass.

a) What was that about? Have you come to peace with your actions? If so, how did you do that?

b) If not, is there anything you can do to come to peace with yourself? Share your story with others.

AGAINST THE ODDS

Huntington Ravine lies on the eastern flank of New Hampshire's Mount Washington. It is a sunny but chilly Easter Sunday morning and a group of us have met to snow and ice climb up the ravine. We are a group of strangers meeting in the Pinkham Notch parking lot, gathering our gear, and packing extra clothing, food and water before beginning the hike into the Hermit Lake shelters. Never having hiked in the winter, this is a new experience for me and I am encouraged by the sunny weather. An uphill hike to the shelters warms us rapidly and we begin peeling layers of clothing as we bask in the warmth of the April sun. Once we gain the shelters we hike north to the foot of Huntington Ravine.

We will be climbing without being roped together. Crampons and ice axe are new equipment for me. Each of us laces crampons, 10-12 pointed metal extensions, onto our boots. I welcome help in figuring out the lacing. These somewhat unwieldy contraptions on the bottom of our boots will help us to dig in as we kick-step up the snow and ice wall, thus protecting us from slipping and falling. Each of us also has an ice axe, to assist both in climbing and in self-arresting in case of a fall. Again this is a new implement for me and some of the others, so we take some moments walking uphill a little ways, lying down on the snow, and allowing ourselves to slide downward as we practice self-arresting with the ice axe. Somewhat practiced, we are ready to go.

Our plan is to climb the ravine to the top of the headwall and then to descend by another route, either the Lion Head or Tuckerman Ravine trail. We begin our ascent. Though we are not roped, we climb together on the wall. Plunging the pointed end of my ice axe into the snow in front of me and holding onto the curved blade, I rely on it to be an anchor securing me to the wall. Stepping forward and upward on my crampons, first right foot and then left, I stabilize myself before lifting the ice axe and plunging it again in the snow, forward and upward of where I stand. This is exhausting! With practice I establish a rhythm. Still it is demanding. I am breathing hard and stop to peel outer layers until I am climbing in a T-shirt and wool pants. Soaked in perspiration, my body cools quickly at each rest stop. Each rest stop also presents other challenges like maintaining balance and keeping all my gear securely in front of me, so it is not lost to the pull of gravity and ends up at the bottom of the ravine!

Together we move upward. As we approach the top of the headwall, we are suddenly enveloped in a full-blown blizzard. Layers of clothing are quickly added—shirts, parka, shell, gloves, hat, and goggles. In a matter of minutes, we go from a sunny Easter Sunday with temperatures above freezing to an arctic blizzard of fierce winds, blowing snow, and wind chill temperatures well below zero.

Now with this blizzard, we can no longer descend by either the Lion Head or Tuckerman Ravine trail due to avalanche danger. Instead we are forced to traverse the entire eastern flank of Mount Washington to descend the Boott Spur, a less steep thus safer route. We travel in single file, being sure to keep the person in front of us within sight so as not to get lost or separated. Probably I should be afraid but I am not, just intensely aware of everything—my breathing, my fatigue, my thirst, the crunch of the icy snow underfoot, staying warm, and the location of the person in front of me. I am also keenly aware of the wind. It is an unremitting constant battering as we traverse. Even more are its sounds—a furious screeching, singing, and moaning—which further exhaust me. "When will we be free of this wind," I wonder. Physical and mental exhaustion set in, and that simply requires more vigilance, since exhaustion and inattention are often preludes to accidents. Finally we reach the Boott Spur and begin our descent. Soon we are below the primary force of the wind but a new challenge appears. With each step forward, crampons must be planted firmly into the snow and ice in order not to slide; however, when doing this, I do not know whether my foot will remain on the surface or sink into an unseen hole that has developed around a hidden boulder. "Post-holing" means sinking up to my hip in snow, struggling to free my leg from the hole, and then continuing my descent with another possible "post hole." This is exhausting. It happens to all of us. Though we move together down the mountain, each of us grapples with his/her own demons; yet no one gives in to the fatigue and whenever possible a helping hand is offered. Dusk comes and we are in full darkness before we reach the trailhead. Never have I been this exhausted.

Together we have gone through the fire and ice of a trial. We came together. On a sunny April day, the mountain became a trickster but we rose to the challenge. A community was created, a community that shepherded each of us through. We were not roped together but we were tethered by our *common ground.*

Reflections

I juxtapose this story with Humbled in the West Shield for this is a North Shield story of wisdom, community, sharing and receiving gifts, gratitude, and wise rational mind. Survival is about being prepared, adapting to conditions, making sound decisions, and staying together. Here there were mature co-leaders who made their gifts known from the outset. They met us eye to eye and checked our gear. I had complete confidence in them. This has not always been my experience. Once caught in the blizzard and having to revise the plan, their wise and rational minds and demeanor gave us confidence and courage for the long trek. They kept us together, and we came together as a community, checking in with one another, watching for frostbite or hypothermia, and cheering on one another despite our exhaustion. We each found gifts that we could bring to one another. Alone we may not have survived the wind, the cold, the snow, or the mountain.

Practices

1) In your family or with a small group of friends or acquaintances, plan an outing to a natural place. Take charge of the planning, organization, and the outing itself. What did you learn? What are the skills you brought to this endeavor? Did anything happen that you did not anticipate? What would you do differently the next time? Is a leader always necessary?

2) Together plan a family or small group outing in which there is no single leader. Take note of how the planning and organizing is accomplished. What gifts can each member bring to the planning and organizing? How might you help those gifts to shine? Go on the outing. How did it go? What were the successes? Problems? Did the family or group function as a community? How was that accomplished? What did you learn?

READING THE RIVER

In March and April, the rivers of the northeast begin to carry snow melt and the time for whitewater enthusiasts is at hand.

We are on a two-day canoeing trip on a river in northwestern Connecticut. We are twelve college students in an outdoor education course and two instructors. In preparation for this trip, the students have been practicing basic canoeing strokes and tandem canoeing on a lake near the campus. All are novice paddlers and campers. It is a cool, cloudy spring weekend—the kind of weather that reminds me that spring is still only a promise. In the early morning cold, camping supplies, food, and extra clothes are stowed in dry bags and divided between the canoes. Tandem canoe pairings are made and we set off onto the river with snow flurries in the air.

The river is wide here and the current slower, giving us time to practice our strokes and get the "feel" of our canoes with the added weight. All seem to be doing well and we head downstream—a parade of canoes with paddlers filled with excitement and trepidation for what lies ahead. As the river narrows and the current increases, we test our skills and learn to "read the river." The lead canoe has an experienced stern paddler to find the best course through the challenges that lie ahead. The last canoe also has an experienced stern paddler. This canoe is called the sweep and is responsible for keeping all other canoes ahead of it on the river. The lead and sweep canoes are like two adult ducks shepherding their young between them.

We hear whitewater before we ever see it. Hearts race with anticipation, idle chatter is displaced by high alert and curt instructions from the stern paddlers. The lead canoe picks the channel with the strongest flow. Paddle power surrenders to the power of the river. Paddles are used to make minor corrections. The lead canoe bobs through the first of the rapids and pulls into a downstream eddy to await the remaining canoes. Those with less experience over-steer, work too hard, or wait too long so their rides are more fraught with anxiety and roughness, but most make it through the baptism of whitewater. The next-to-last canoe gets crosswise to the current and heads into the whitewater broadside. A boulder looms and the bow seems to be racing to meet it. At the last moment, backstrokes and water team to push the bow away from the boulder and the canoe bounces backward through the whitewater. All are safe and dry. Some are exhilarated while others are shaken. The first of the whitewater has been met, and we ease our canoes into the backwater eddy to collect ourselves before moving down the river.

Reflections

This is a North Shield story. Learning to work with all the elements of a community, whether human or otherwise, demands maturity, trust, surrender, appreciation of one's own gifts and limitations as well as the gifts and limitations of others, patience, wisdom, and a desire for harmony.

Whitewater canoeing is like learning to dance with a partner. First, there is the dance with the other person in the canoe. One person leads. In canoeing that is the stern paddler for that is the power position in the canoe. Though each paddler needs to have command of the strokes, the bow paddler has to be willing to respond to the commands of the stern paddler. The skills and attitude that each brings to this endeavor will determine both their success in partnering as well as their success in negotiating the white water challenges. Once a team has experienced white water several times, there is a seamless play of respective skills and knowing with little or no verbal communication.

There is a second dance occurring. This is the dance between the paddlers and the river. This, too, is a partnership. One can see the river as an enemy to be attacked. To do so will eventually teach one that the river is more powerful than one's muscle. The partnership is in learning to "read the river," to meet it on its terms, and to allow the power of the river to guide one. The more proficient one becomes in "reading the river" and the more finely tuned the skills, the bigger whitewater challenges one can take on with success.

And the third dance is that between the river and its surroundings. The river is a living being. It has found a path of least resistance in its journey to the sea. Despite the flow of whitewater governed by season, there are places on the river where peace and stillness reside—the downstream and backwater eddies. It is often difficult to see these places among the tumult of whitewater. But look directly below a river or stream boulder and you will find a quiet pocket of water. You might see leaves or sticks floating there. Paddlers can turn into such an eddy with bow upstream and gather themselves for the next whitewater run. When ready, paddlers turn the bow out into the current and the canoe turns 180 degrees and joins the downstream flow once again. This is not unlike those times in our own lives when we need to stop and take a breath and integrate new learnings and understandings before we reenter the fray. This behavior in personal growth, in relationships, and in all creative endeavors is very healthy.

Practices

1) Go out to a watercourse where the water is flowing. Watch its flow and how it negotiates the obstacles.

   a) If you were riding on this watercourse, choose the route you would take. Now let a stick or leaf become your boat and surrender it to the water. Where does it go and how does it meet obstacles?

   b) How do this stream and the stick/leaf become metaphors for your life? What do the stream and the stick/leaf have to teach you about surrender, partnership, relentlessness, stillness?

2) How do you work as a member of a team—family, partner, work mates, sports team, etc.?

    a) When does a shared goal override your individual goal?

    b) When is it difficult for you to surrender your own need to be recognized or heard by the group? When is it not difficult? Why? How do you decide? Who helps you with this? Do you ask for the help or is it proffered? Which do you prefer? What is the message here for you?

3) When the flow is going downstream for you and you suddenly feel yourself crosswise to the stream or even paddling upstream, what are your choices? Think about the watercourse—surrender, fight harder, look for a resting place, leave the river, capsize, ask for help.

4) Go out into nature to accomplish a task together as a family or group, for example camping, hiking, a cross-country ski trip, canoeing, building or repairing a trail, etc. How can you make this a community venture both in preparation and action? How does the team solve problems? How are decisions made? Are there times when community decisions are inappropriate? If so, when? If not, why not?

NAMING AND KNOWING

In my twenties when I first began to reconnect with the natural world, I always had a destination in mind, usually a backcountry lake or a mountain peak. It was the goal that was important and I afforded little attention to the flora or fauna on the way to my goal. Of course, as a visitor I missed much along the way. Since that time, I have met many who attack the outdoors in similar manner. Like me of old, they see, really see, little of what they pass through. For both of us, the wilderness was treated as an "It," something to be conquered.

The writing of many nature writers and the guidance of mentors taught me another way of being in the natural world. Here are some remembrances.

There was a colleague/friend who was a birder. I knew the common birds indigenous to where I grew up—robins, starlings, red wings, blue jays, etc.—but she knew many more and she could identify them by size, color, song, wing bars, and eye rings. Eye rings? I had never looked that closely before. It was a new challenge to scan a tree with binoculars following a moving bird to really study it and identify it. But it did not stop there. My curiosity led me to habitat, nesting patterns, flight patterns, and food sources, so my knowing expanded beyond naming.

Another colleague/friend introduced me to the west. We were car camping and doing short walks. She knew many of the plants which were completely foreign to me. And I found that there were guides to flowers and plants just like the guides to birds.

During one of my first summers in the west, I camped at the Maroon Bells outside of Aspen, Colorado. Each day I would hike through a meadow to get to the mountains. One day instead of hiking, I decided to spend the afternoon in the meadow using a new flower guide to identify flowers. First, I had to familiarize myself with how the guide was organized. OK, start with color. Then I realize flowers come in shapes! Why haven't I noticed this before? Once narrowing a flower down to color and shape, I needed to consider height of the plant, how leaves are organized on the stem, and other small details. In two hours of exploration, I sat on many rocks, paged through sections of the guide many times, identified several flowers, and traveled not very far. What I discovered was that I was no longer just looking, but really seeing. The closer I got to each flower, the more I saw, and the deeper my connection to each flower and the entire meadow. There was growing joy in this process of traversing the meadow day after day: naming flowers; studying them in the sun or shade or early morning dew, nestled and sheltered by rocks; or standing tall as if to say, "here I am, come notice me." In subsequent years, those few hours of study continue to bring pure joy when I greet these familiar friends elsewhere in nature.

Then there was a guide who taught me about hiking pace. My first experience with him was on a climb of Long's Peak in Colorado. We were on the trail by 4 a.m.

and we hiked uphill for three hours without stopping. We stopped only because there was someone in the party who asked for a rest. I realized that with his pace, I did not need to stop frequently to catch my breath before proceeding, even at 12,000 feet and beyond. But it was not just about pace. He had a rhythm. There was no stopping and starting and no hesitation as the trail steepened. He maintained a steadiness and fluidity regardless of the obstacles. He seemed to be looking a few steps ahead, always planning where each foot would be placed so that a rhythm could be maintained. He effortlessly "fit" himself to the terrain. What a gift to me who was expert at "attacking" the trail. This was a revelation and completely altered how I hiked. Hiking became a walking meditation. There was deliberateness, sureness of foot, steadiness of pace, and a flow, which set me free to be in the natural world.

Reflections

Naming brings order. Though naming allows for organizing and establishing some control over one's environment, it only objectifies. Birds, flowers, trees, or people remain "it." In looking beyond merely naming, we can deepen our connection to the world around us—both natural and human. How easily we resort to names to categorize—Catholic, Jew, Muslim, African American, Native American, Redneck, Schizo, Sped, Gay, or Lesbian. These are just names without knowing. It keeps us separate from one another on this planet.

Here I moved from the South Shield of total disregard for what was around me, to meeting what I did not know (West Shield), to a deeper knowing (North Shield). It was as if I were building friendships with the flowers, the birds, and the trails. I found that as I came to know more about the environment through which I was wandering, the deeper my experience. In doing so, I became less an intruder and more a fellow being.

Practices

1) Depending on the season, use a guide to identify some aspect of the natural world—birds, water fowl, trees, animal tracks, flowers, insects, stars, etc. Find a place to sit, watch, and listen. You may find you will need some added equipment—magnifying glass, binoculars, boots, or cushion. Bring them next time. Allow yourself to be drawn into your surroundings. Bring curiosity and patience. Identify what you can. Pay attention to what is happening to you as you are drawn in. Name but go deeper. Read more about who you meet. Consider how the one you name fits into the Circle of Life.

2) In a small group, select someone you do not know. Take 20 minutes to get to know something about this person. Try to avoid details like where

one lives or what one does for work, and focus instead on a deeper knowing.

After 20 minutes, switch roles. When finished, take a few minutes to journal about this experience. Share your thoughts. What have you learned about yourself? About meeting others?

3) Now bring the skill of seeing and the attributes of curiosity, courage, and patience into the human world. What happens to you when you allow yourself to see another beyond the label of name, race, faith, or gender? This is not easy. Pay attention to your fears of the unknown. What do you need to do to meet your fear? Can you break it down into small steps? Where can you do this? Do you need help? Practice bringing curiosity, rather than judgment, into the process.

MEETING WILDLIFE

It's the last night of camping in the Colorado Rockies before driving east. Hunkered down in a small camp chair, enjoying a fire in the fire ring and the quiet of the evening, my campsite suddenly comes alive with excited, pleading calls from a clutch of young robins that fledged earlier in the day. Mother robin is clucking. I think she is trying to get them to a safe roosting spot for the night. Wings flap wildly but the young robins swoop downward, not upward! One of the young, beating its wings frantically, lands on the edge of the fire ring, teeters precariously, and finally jumps to safety. Inevitably each lands on the ground, instead of in a tree. Each is frantically peeping while mother robin clucks encouragement and instructions. A young robin hops beneath my camp chair. Clearly, I am in the flight pattern! I try not to move but my head is swiveling as I watch this dance evolve. Filled with joy and hope, I secretly and fervently pray for safety from nighttime harm.

As dusk settles, no fledgling has made it to safety despite the mother's encouragement. Each flaps, peeps, pleads, but not one can accomplish upward flight. Finally, the mother flies to a tree trunk that is atilt and calls the young robins to her. Each gets to the base of the trunk then flutters, hops, and walks its way up to safety; all but one. Repeatedly it tries to climb, only to fall backward, seemingly exhausted. The mother's calls become more strident. Finally with darkness, all becomes silent. With mother's single cluck, the peeping fledgling quiets and settles at the base of the tree. I leave them be, let my campfire burn down then retire to my tent. With dawn, there is a raucous leave taking long before I arise to pack and drive home.

On another trip west, I am on the last day of a backpacking trip. Rounding a hairpin turn on the trail, I come face to face with a grouse and her young brood. I am in a rhythm, focused on getting back to the trailhead, and dreaming of the ice cream soda I will have when I get to town, so I push on rather than stop; but mother grouse has other ideas. She charges at me with wings flapping. Stunned, I screech to a halt while trying to reassure her that I mean no harm. Of course, she does not respond to English! She charges again and I begin to retreat. During all of this, she is clucking and her young are peeping. Then the grouse turns, flaps her wings as if injured, and limps down the trail. I am mesmerized and my attention is totally focused on her. Suddenly there are no chicks and not a peep to be heard. Mother grouse has successfully gained my total attention while directing her young into hiding. There is only stillness. She heads down the trail and I follow slowly. She turns off into the undergrowth, eventually to double back and collect her brood. I continue down the trail with less swagger, more presence, and gratitude for her teaching.

Reflections

I have juxtaposed these two stories—one of the North Shield, the other of the South Shield. For me there has always been the need to be part of, rather than being apart from, the natural world. There is deep satisfaction in being in the natural world and having the natural world receive me without skittering away. To stand beside a moose foraging on the trail, to have a deer lick the salts of perspiration from my hand, to have a bald eagle plunge into the water beside my canoe, to stand eye to eye with a rattlesnake—these are memories etched in the emulsion of my mind. To me, these are North Shield experiences. They are of essence meeting essence. I honor their being and, in return, find myself being honored rather than being feared. For many years this has been easier for me to do in the natural world than in the everyday human world. But in the ongoing travels around the Medicine Wheel, this, too, becomes easier.

When I am lost in myself and not present in my environment, then I am in the South Shield of "I." This was the case when I met grouse. Stuck in my rhythm and unwilling to stop, I did not honor her. I could have stopped rather than plowing forward. How different would have been our meeting? There was a teaching in my self-absorption but I missed out on a true meeting of essences.

Practices

1) Go out in spring in the early morning or late afternoon, listen, and watch for birds. Watch for patterns of flight and see if you can locate a nest. Watch from afar. Remember this place. Visit it daily until the young are fledged. If you are lucky you might be witness to the fledging.

2) Find a place in the natural world that you can visit often—a favorite tree, a pond, woodland stream, or meadow, for example. Find a place to sit, listen, and watch. Develop micro, middle distance, and far distance vision. Become part of the landscape.

   a) What happens right next to you? Who comes to visit? Who scampers? Who stalks?
   b) Who lives here? Who passes through?
   c) When does essence meet essence?

3) In the world of humans, take note:

   a) What does it mean to be fully present? When do you experience that? What gets in the way of being fully present?
   b) What work can you do in the West Shield that may help you to move into the North Shield?

GIFTS THAT SUSTAIN

Canadian geese hold a special place in my heart. Always, their call stirs both my memories and my very being.

- One early spring, an injured goose leaves its migrating flock and lands at our farm. It stays at our small pond through the summer and early autumn. It rests, heals, forages, and keeps a solitary existence. It is much kinder to us children than the three white geese that often chase us around the yard. Wary at first, it gradually comes closer when we shake the corn pail. It is a wonderful addition to our little pond. Then one October day, the calls of a southward-flying flock summon it skyward, never to return to us. Though I merely wave farewell, I secretly wish I could go, too.

- One moonlit night deep in the Grand Canyon, we are all awakened by the honking of eight Canadian geese flying low over the Colorado River. Their honking, echoing off the canyon walls, creates a cacophony worthy of eighty! There is something primal about this wilderness experience in a place of such ancient wonder. This is the anniversary of John Wesley Powell's first trip down the Colorado, so all along the way we read excerpts from his journals. Also we see the evidence of the Anasazi who once lived in these canyons. Somehow the calls of the geese

link us all—past, present and future. A great
swelling of harmony and peace infuses my entire
being as I drift back to sleep.

• What truly enchants me is the actual spring and
fall migrations. I am in complete wonder of that
characteristic "V" passing overhead. I catch sight of
the seamless "changing of the guard" as the tiring
leader drops back to the end of the line to ride
in the slipstream as a new leader moves forward
to "break trail." What a neat idea, and I marvel at
how this has been worked out over time while
also wondering what we might learn from this.

The clarion calls of the geese reach deep inside me
and my urge is to take flight and go with them. They
feel like my ancestors. I know that the migrating urge
lives in my DNA, holding the memory of my earliest
ancestors, who moved with the seasons. That urge
holds, too, the memory of my grandparents, who left
the Old World to risk the New World. The longing to
fly rises each time I hear that distinctive call. It stops
me in my tracks. I listen intently and scan the sky for
that "V." I wave. "Take me with you," I call. But being
only human, I am earthbound and can only wish them
"good speed." Still my spirit longs to fly with them.

Reflections

This is a North Shield story of gifts. The Canadian Geese
bring gifts to me and I, in turn, share the gift of story.

It is a story of the ancestors and community that exists through the ages. And it is a story of opening oneself more deeply to community. In our deepest being, we are all one. Our human ancestors learned from their environment. Their—and consequently our—survival depended upon keen observation and the ability to transmute knowledge into action. Critical to survival was the sustainability of community through protecting and teaching the young, transitioning into adulthood, working together in hunting and gathering, sharing food, and honoring the elders. We have remained faithful to many of these ideas as it relates to our family or tribe. But sustainability is not a concept that we have nurtured well when we consider both the human species or the Web of Life. With respect to the human species, there are clear divisions between the haves and the have nots when it comes to such attributes as color, gender, religion, sex, education, and income, among others. And when we consider all beings on this planet, we have turned a blind eye to what our ancestors knew and what today's indigenous people know. When we forget our ancestors and the commitment to sustainable community, we endanger ourselves because we and the planet are one.

Practices

1) Is there some being in the natural world with whom you already feel some affinity?

a) If so, what draws you to it—sound, color, myth, how it moves, where it lives, how it lives, etc.? Reflect on your connection to it. How did that start? What has been the journey? What meaning does this being hold for you in your life? What is it here to teach you about you, community, and your place in it? Get to know this being even more intimately—sit with it, be with it through the seasons and in different weather. Study it in any way that seems helpful to you but remember to do it no harm. How did it get here in this time and place? Who are its ancestors?

b) If there is no being in the natural world with whom you feel an affinity, then let's begin to find one. Consider the flora and fauna. Is there a plant, a flower, a tree, or an animal to which you are drawn? If not, then go out into the natural world and let that being come to you as you wander. Be open to whatever being shows up. Then sit with this being in its natural setting and back home. Why has this being come to you? What do you know about it? Where did it come from? How did it get here in this time and place? Who are its ancestors? What is it here to teach you about you, community, and your place in it? Get to know it even more intimately.

2) What connection did your ancestors have to this being? What would they like you to know about this being? What new knowledge about this being do you want to carry forth to those yet to be born?

3) Create a way to celebrate this being in your life—a story, a poem, a picture, a collage, whatever helps you to hold its presence inside you.

4) What are the gifts of your ancestors to you? List them. Share them with others.

5) What are the gifts you bring to the world and for those who will follow? List them. Share them.

CHAPTER SEVEN

Coming Full Circle—Traveling the Blue Road of Death and Transformation

When the oak is felled the whole forest echoes with its fall, but a hundred acorns are sown in silence by an unnoticed breeze.

Thomas Carlyle

Doesn't everything die at last, and too soon?
Tell me, what is it you plan to do
with your one wild and precious life?

From "The Summer Day" by
Mary Oliver in *New and Selected Poems*

A TRIP AROUND THE WHEEL

After hiking miles each day on my summer vacations in the Rocky Mountains, I decide to try backpacking so I can get deeper into the backcountry. Knowing nothing about backpacking but wanting to learn, I sign-up for a group-sponsored backpacking trip in southwestern Colorado. It is an eight-day trip. The sponsoring group is reputable and I think this will be the safest way to learn. We meet early one morning at the trailhead. There are two co-leaders and ten packers. We meet, divide up the community gear—food, pots and pans—weigh our packs to be sure they are not too heavy, and head out onto the trail. The planned trek into the backcountry is a circle route over a series of passes, with one or more base camps, while exploring and summiting 14,000-foot peaks before returning to the trailhead.

Excited about this adventure and the opportunity to learn the ins and outs of backpacking safely, I am ready to put my life in the hands of these two co-leaders. For most of the first day, the trail parallels a river that runs on our left. In the late afternoon, we must cross this river in order to continue. There is no bridge. The river is rushing along with rain and snowmelt from the surrounding high peaks. The leaders explain to us how we will ford this river and proceed with the set-up. Taking out a climbing rope, they anchor one end to a tree on the shore on which we stand and we watch as one leader, braving the icy cold current, carries the other end of the rope across to the far river bank, and anchors it to a tree there. Now, one at a time, each of us fords the river holding onto this rope stretched between the two banks. We have been instructed to take off our hiking boots to keep them dry, and to unbuckle the waist belt of our pack, so that we can shuck the pack should we fall into the river. During the hike into this place, I had become acutely aware of the weight of my pack and how easily it can act to destabilize me if I shift my weight too quickly. Now I learn that if I fall into the water, my pack will become an anchor serving to drown me if I cannot get free of it!

Watching with mounting anxiety, the first packers inch their way, one by one, across the river. No one falls; however, I note how little stability the rope offers as it swings up and down, back and forth, as each person seeks its wobbly protection. Finally, it is my turn. With my boots tied together and hanging around my neck, I unbuckle my pack, ease my way into the water, and seek secure footing. My breath catches as my feet and legs hit the icy cold water. The current is strong, much stronger than I anticipated. Clutching the rope with my right hand, I begin my crossing totally focused on not drowning and reaching the other side. The rocks underfoot are sharp and the water is above my knees. Though moving with caution, I am also aware of how much I want to get this over. My feet hurt and, in my mind's eye, I see them cut up and bloodied by the jagged rocks. Numb with cold, I emerge on the far bank unscathed. I am simply amazed. I am also beginning to wonder if there may have been an easier

way to ford this river, but I do not know how. I wonder
if our lives were put at unnecessary risk but, then again,
what do I know as a neophyte backpacker?

We collect ourselves and make camp here. It is July
1969. The moon is coming into its fullness and we
know that Apollo XI may be on its way to the moon.
We sit around this wilderness campfire and speculate
about men on the moon! Soon I retire to my tent still
musing about the river crossing.

The next morning we breakfast, pack up, and set
out to climb up to and across a 12,000-foot pass, then
drop down into a valley where we will base camp
for a few days. Usually passes are approached via a
series of switchbacks which lengthen hiking distances
but reduce steepness. There is no trail up to the pass
and the leaders are taking us straight up, huffing and
puffing beneath the load we carry on our backs.

Weather on the western side of the Continental
Divide is wetter than on the eastern side. Since the
movement of weather fronts is hindered by the Divide,
here clouds and rain can settle in for a few days. As
we ascend the pass, a storm approaches from the west.
I can feel the electricity building in the air. Lightning
lurks. The leaders know this but we push ever higher.
One of the leaders passes along the word that we
should stand on our right leg if lightning strikes so that
the bolt will pass down the right side of one's body and
thus miss the heart! Now I know the leadership of this
group is in trouble and so are all of us. I am a teacher.
I have taught first aid. How dumb is this? Fortunately,

the weather holds off, we reach the pass. Just we as begin to descend, one of the leaders offers a challenge to see who will get to the base camp first. Of course the youngest member of the party, an unaccompanied twelve-year-old takes up the challenge, begins running downhill, falls, and sprains an ankle. This slows us up. I know what I am thinking but say nothing. We arrive at base camp in the rain.

The next day is overcast, cool, and wet. The co-leaders offer to lead a climb of a 14,000-foot peak. Tired, annoyed, and not feeling very kindly towards these leaders, I elect to remain in camp to relax, explore, and think. There is a thunderstorm during the day. When the group returns, I learn from hikers that the leaders left them sitting on a false peak in the thunderstorm, while the leaders went on to "bag" the real 14,000-foot peak! Later that afternoon, the leaders announce that the circle route they had planned will have to be aborted due to snow fields. I assume they saw that from their 14,000-foot perch. The plan is to remain at this base camp, hike from here for a few days, and then return to the trailhead via the same route we used on the way in. Disappointed and angry, I realize that I no longer need others, especially these leaders, to teach me about backpacking, and resolve to leave.

To leave means having to ford the river again. Cautiously, I begin talking with others to find if anyone else is similarly disgruntled. Quickly I find another wishing to leave. We talk about leaving together, discuss how to ford the river, and when to approach the leaders.

After dinner, we approach the group leaders who try to dissuade us. We are resolute. We know they cannot stop us. Discussion continues and finally they reluctantly agree but make two requirements. First, we must sign a paper releasing the leaders from any responsibility should anything befall us and, second, we are not to tell anyone until breakfast the next morning. Clearly they anticipate a mutiny and, foolishly, we agree to keep our counsel until the next morning.

Next morning at breakfast, we break the news. As we pack up our gear, several trip members come to us quietly to tell us they would like to be going out with us. We say our farewells and head out onto the trail. Our plan is to cover in one long day what the group has covered in two days. Our biggest worry is the river. During our hike, we discuss several plans for crossing the river and settle upon a single plan. My partner decides to wear his sneakers and I decide to tie my moccasins to my feet to make the ford easier. We decide to cross as partners. Side by side we hold our adjacent hands—right to left. One of us remains stationary while the other moves forward; then the person in front remains stationary, while the person behind moves ahead and takes up a stationary position, allowing the one behind to move forward, and so on. Thus we are moving together but always from a stable base of support. We cross easily and quickly. We are proud both of our problem-solving and our action. And now we are ever more resolute about our decision to leave the trip. We hike out without incident.

Reflections

It has been a long time since I have thought about this trip. My feet have covered many miles since then. Most of us were beings living in the South Shield when it came to backpacking. We were seeking leadership based on knowledge and wisdom. Instead we had leaders who were stuck somewhere between the South Shield of "I" and the West Shield of "I am." In other words, their desire to climb 14,000 foot peaks, called "peak bagging," was primary and leading this backpacking trip into an area of many such peaks made it, financially, a free trip for the leaders. In the process, our lives were put at greater risk than necessary.

This is a full Medicine Wheel story beginning in the East Shield and moving around the Wheel to return to the east. First, I wanted to test myself beyond that of day hikes and wanted to go more deeply into the wilderness. Wanting to birth myself into a new part of my journey in the natural world, I knew I needed help with equipment, packing, weight distribution, hiking with a backpack, and finding physical limits, so I moved to the South Shield. I put myself in the hands of those more experienced and more knowledgeable. Then as we moved from the fording of the river, to the ascent to the pass in an impending storm, to a breakneck descent to base camp, to peak bagging, and then to the route change, I was plunged into the West Shield. Having to acknowledge to myself that I was not in a safe environment under this leadership, I had to begin to honor the knowledge and skills I had developed while hiking. I had to trust my instincts and claim my voice to venture into the unknown, both in finding a like-minded partner and in leaving the group. These all speak to moving into the West Shield. Finding another and working together to problem-solve were steps into the North Shield. Had I been psychically stronger, I would have raised my concerns, questions, and doubts in the full community at base camp. Then I would have been fully in the North Shield. I do not know what happened to the group after we left. Perhaps the community found its voice. This single backpacking experience freed me to take on new backpacking challenges, which provided still more trips around the Medicine Wheel; each offering new experiences, an ending, and a new beginning.

My very next backpacking trip was a solo overnight to Jim's Grove on the eastern slopes of Long's Peak in Colorado. There was the challenge of going alone. This meant meeting the sounds of the darkness—the incessant winds, little creatures scampering around and on my tent, and bigger creatures sniffing around my little tent. It was the heard but unseen which frightened me. So I took a transistor radio to muffle the sounds which would keep me awake! Surviving the night, the experience freed me to leave the radio at home the next time, so that I could welcome the night and its sounds and feel safe within the walls of my tent. Another circle completed, each freeing me to explore ever deeper into the wilderness.

Practices

1) As you move more fully out into the natural world, be mindful of the knowledge and skills you are learning in each experience. Watch how each experience allows you to try something a little different the next time, e.g. walk further, go into a new area, get closer to something of which you are unsure.

2) Share a passion of yours with a small group, e.g. teach them something you love, lead them on a walk or short trip. How do you balance your needs with those of the group? Be mindful of 1) when you are in the South Shield of ego and "I"; 2) when you enter the West Shield of letting go of the known and allowing the experience to evolve for all; and 3) when you enter the North Shield of allowing the community to emerge. Note what this frees you to do with your passion as you move into the East Shield.

3) Reflect on a time in a group when you were stuck in an exaggerated South Shield of "I", when you were focused only on yourself and not the others. Why were you stuck or what would you have had to let go of in order to move forward? If you let go, how did you accomplish that? Did anyone help you? What evolved as a result? If you could not let go, what happened? What did you learn that helped you in the future?

MEETING SPIRIT

A friend and I are in the Yosemite backcountry. We have packed over a ridge and down to a high alpine lake. We set up camp, cook dinner, eat, and clean up. Each of us wanders off for time alone as the soft light of evening approaches. Absorbed in looking down successive valleys to Half Dome in the western distance, in the quickness of a moment I am transported to another time and place. Leaving behind all thoughts of the day, I find myself wondering why I am here on the planet in this time and place. Like a photograph slowly developing in its chemical bath, an image develops in my mind—I see a long slender thread that reaches back to the earliest ancestors, spans eons of time to the present, and continues into the time yet to come. I am just a speck on this thread. Everyone is a speck on this thread. Each of us is part of this thread. Without me, without you, the thread would not continue. My mere presence and yours adds to the thread. Weeping with the relief of knowing this, I am filled with an immense joy of connectedness to all those who have gone before me as well as a sacredness to know that I am holding a gift for those who follow. I am filled with a deep peace.

Reflections

Spirit comes to me in the wilderness. I cannot make it happen. Believe me, I have tried! With time and maturity, I have learned to relax, to open myself to the present and the presence of others, whatever "other" means. I do not pretend to know. All I know is that I must "show up." I must be aware and present in the moment. I am also sure that spirit has come to me in moments when I have not been present and missed it entirely! Certainly this has happened to me in the everyday human world. Slowly, I am learning that I do not have to be in the wilderness to have spirit make itself known. More and more I meet it in others. What it requires of me is an openness, a vulnerability, a curiosity, a stripping away of my defenses, and a trust in myself. As I honor my place on the thread, I honor another's. Together we weave the thread.

With this story I come full circle. In traveling the blue road of death and letting go of a belief that held me back, I allowed spirit to touch me in new and deeper ways. It freed me to leave behind a measure of self-doubt, so I could more fully embrace my gifts and bring them into the world of community. Now another journey around the Medicine Wheel begins.

Practices

1) Where do you encounter spirit? What helps you to do that? What holds you back?

2) Why are you here? What are your gifts to your community?

3) What gifts have you received from the ancestors?

4) How can you help others to claim their gifts?

FULL CIRCLE

I am participating in a workshop at The School of Lost Borders in eastern California. We are nearing the end of our time together and, for our last experience, each of us is asked to go out into the wilderness to have a conversation with a non-human being and to return with the conversation. Immediately I know where I will go and the time of day I will choose.

The next morning, well before dawn, I dress, unzip my tent, leave the campground in my car, and drive to the Bristlecone Pine Forest east of Big Pine. My intention is to spend the sunrise with one of the old matriarchs, the oldest living trees on Earth. I know the tree I will come to, for a few days before the workshop I had come to this forest and walked a few of its trails. Filled with anticipation, I am anxious to get to the trailhead and race the car along the winding road. Finally the parking lot comes into view. At 12,000 feet it is a crisp, chilly predawn and hurriedly I put on extra layers including winter hat and gloves. I am carrying with me a Medicine Wheel I had made of native materials earlier in the workshop. Not really knowing why I am bringing it, I listen to the compelling voice that says, "Bring it."

The path climbs steadily upward to my destination. Breathing hard, I do not want to take the time to rest. Soon the tree comes into view. As I climb up to the east side of the tree, the dawning light unfolds on this matriarch, and the sun's first rays catch the High Sierra peaks in the distance. I love being here. This matriarch is three-quarters dead and one-quarter alive. Already she has lived much of her life as have I.

Here I stand unsure of what to do next. Waiting. What comes to me is the urge to lie down, to prostrate myself on the rocks at the foot of this tree. Despite being discomfited by this thought, I do it and am immediately filled with emotion that arises from somewhere deep inside me. The uneven ground, the rocks, the cold do not distract me. Through tears, I begin my conversation.

I offer a prayer of gratitude:

"Ancient One, thank you for your presence, your stamina, your roots, your courage and your witnessing of life."

The Ancient One responds:

"But these are your qualities, too. You may be a child in the universe but you are an elder in the community of humans."

I ask:

"What can you tell me about living and dying?"

She responds:

"I have nothing to offer."

I understand. My questions then turn to the tree herself:

"I see all these scars upon you. Can you tell me about them?"

The Ancient One answers:

"These scars hold the story of my life. They make me an individual among the other tress. They give me character and, in time, these scars become marks of beauty."

I tell her:

"Since I first came to visit the Ancient Ones several years ago, I knew that this is where my ashes will come when I die. I cannot think of a more honored place to be with the ancestors."

The Ancient One says:

"I will welcome your ashes to rest with the Ancients."

She goes on:

"These parts of me that have already died represent not only my great age but also all the destruction that I have witnessed in the world—the destruction caused by natural upheavals as well as the destruction wrought by humans through the ages. I have suffered the destruction of the Earth and her precious resources and the torture and slaughter of one another. The time is short. Do what you can to bring peace and harmony."

Deeply moved by both her presence and her message, I respond:

"Thank you for honoring me as an elder. I will do my best to bring my gifts to my community."

I remain prostrate for a few more minutes then rise to my feet. Laying my Medicine Wheel on her trunk, slowly I disassemble the Wheel. I lay the sage at the base of this Ancient One. Taking each of the stones representing the four shields, I drop them—red, black, white, gold—one at a time into a hole in her trunk returning the stones to the earth just as my ashes will return one day. I no longer need the symbol of the Medicine Wheel, for the Wheel lives within me.

Feeling complete and full, I return to our group with my conversation.

Reflections

This is a Blue Road story—that part of the Medicine Wheel where surrender and letting go occurs so that something new can be birthed. When I started out, I had no idea what would happen. I do not participate in an organized religion believing religion, as it is practiced, to be a great source of divisiveness in the world. Yet here I was prostrating myself before this Bristlecone Pine. That in itself was a huge letting go of ego, of always needing to do it by myself, of opening myself to vulnerability, and then sharing that with others.

Further, the conversation reflected a major step forward in claiming my elderhood and the gifts I need to bring forward into my community.

Lastly, in disassembling the Medicine Wheel, I was acknowledging the need to no longer be attached to a symbol. Once a teaching is made manifest internally, the symbol becomes unnecessary.

All three of these experiences (the prostration, the conversation, and the letting go of symbol) brought me to the East Shield, the place of transformation and new beginnings. Together they were part of one story—a woman going out to find a non-human being with whom to have a conversation.

Practices

1) Go out and find a non-human being with whom to have a conversation

   a) Bring your conversation back to share with a trusted other or the group you are in.
   b) Reflect on what this encounter has to teach you about your location on the Medicine Wheel and what your next growth step might be.

2) What belief about yourself is it time to let go of so that you may embrace something new?

3) What symbol or material object are you willing to free yourself of? Why? How will this free you?

4) What plans have you made for your body when you die? Will parts be recycled? Will you be cremated? Will you be buried in a casket? Will you have a natural burial? What beliefs underlie your decision?

CHAPTER EIGHT

Some Thoughts On Building Community

What pattern connects the crab to the lobster to the orchid to the primrose and four of them to me? And me to you? And all six of us to the amoeba in one direction and the backward schizophrenic in another?

Gregory Bateson,
Mind & Nature: A Necessary Unity

Real maturity is the ability to imagine the humanity of every person as fully as you believe in your own humanity.

Tobias Wolff

When first imagining this book, I had no plans for including a specific chapter concerning community. In the process of writing, what has become clear to me is the significance of community if we are to survive. When I think deeply about this, ultimately we are always seeking balanced and healthy community.

First, there is the community within the self. The stories herein demonstrate how I am forever moving through the Four Shields of the Medicine Wheel. From the inspiration and excitement of new beginnings in the East Shield, to the innocence and ego of the South Shield, to the introspection and darkness of the West, to the wisdom and sharing in the North, and back to refinement and transformation in the East, I am ever seeking a dynamic balance. If the Medicine Wheel could be seen as a horizontal disc balanced on a pin, we seek balance between the east and west (the light and the dark, the masculine and feminine); and the south and the north (the I and the we, childhood and adulthood) as we engage in our daily activities and relationships. Balance here does not imply stasis. The disc, to maintain balance on the pin, is slowly spinning in a wavelike pattern with each dip showing where one is located on the Medicine Wheel. Conceived in this manner, the question becomes, "How do I keep this community within me in dynamic balance so as to continue to grow and manifest my potential?"

Second, there is the community without—the several communities of which I am a member from the micro of family to the macro of the planet. In the stories herein in which others are present (Against the Odds, A Sense of Wonder, Letting Go, Being in Silence, and Reading the River), I and everyone else on the trip is moving around his/her own Medicine Wheel. At the same time, all of us are moving around a second Medicine Wheel—a group wheel. In other words, each group of which you or I are a member undergoes passage through the Four Shields. Thus groups form, meet challenges, enter the darkness, get stuck or grow into mature entities, and then travel the blue road of death and transformation as circumstances and membership changes. Functioning groups are not static and are constantly challenged to seek dynamic balance, just as we do as individuals. Here the question becomes, "What are my responsibilities in helping the groups of which I am a member to mature and remain open to change?"

Third, wherever I am located in these stories (A Great Turning, Into the Darkness and Unknown, Naming and Knowing), I am part of a much larger community, that of all the plants, animals, rocks, water, earth, and air in my surroundings. In Fire and Transformation, I am walking nature's blue road of death and destruction, yet I find underfoot the birth of the new life of the East Shield. In Humbled, I am experiencing my own darkness and terror while all around me nature's beings are also being assaulted by the gods of wind and rain. Here the question becomes, "How do I live on this planet not as a visitor but as someone who respects all that is here knowing that what is here is all there is?"

With these three perspectives in mind—self, human community, planet—I reflect back on my life and ask myself what I have learned and where do I go from here.

1) What essences must I continue to nurture in myself to keep my own internal Medicine Wheel in dynamic balance?
2) What have I learned about groups and their structures that contributes to a group's being able to mature while maintaining openness to transformation?
3) What can I/we do to live on this planet not as visitors but as stewards of all of life?

Throughout this book, the stories, reflections, and practices have been opportunities to help you, the reader, and in turn, those whom you touch, to continue moving ever around the Medicine Wheel, until your physical life on this planet comes to an end and you are transformed. How each of us chooses to do this is a great adventure open to each of us. There is no single model, nor is there a single path. It is both exciting and daunting to truly know that it is up to each of us to create his/her path to peace and harmony. Regardless of the path, each of us must uncover the answers to these life-giving questions if we are to survive individually and collectively.

What essences must I nurture within myself?

I know there are a variety of ways to allow fear to get in the way of my moving forward around the Medicine Wheel. Fear can be found everywhere on the Wheel, for to move from one Shield to another I must let go of the security of the known to enter the unknown. There is the unknown within me, the unknown in relationships, and the unknown in the world. If I can live in the security of a cocoon, I am not challenged to look inward to see my darkness, my blind spots, my judgments, and the fears of what I will uncover. By clinging to what I have, what I know, and what comforts me, even if it is not healthy, I can keep at bay my worst fears about myself—my limitations, my narcissism, my arrogance, and my worthlessness. Through negative experiences in family, schooling, peer groups, teams, and work places, I created defenses and excuses to protect me from risking the unknowns of life. How many of these are familiar to you?

I'm not good enough. I'm different. Who am I to speak up? I'm better than . . . . ! I would not know what to say. It's not my problem. I don't have the time. What will happen if they think I'm stupid? Or someone gets mad at me? Or I lose my friends? Or they don't like what I have to say? Or they laugh at me? Or they want more from me than I can give? Or I have to work with someone who is a talker, boring, conservative, liberal, prejudiced?

Regardless of where on the Medicine Wheel I encounter my fear, I must have the **courage** to let go of an old belief and surrender into a new experience. Repeatedly I have had to take another step forward into the void to find the truth of my own being. Over a life time, each of us faces many challenges, many losses, and sometimes traumas, yet we have survived. This is the courage borne of survival. It takes great courage to consciously and deliberately decide to act, to step forward into the unknown. This is not courage borne of reaction and our will to survive, but courage to proactively meet and embrace our fear to move into full embodied living.

Here it is useful to **remember** the numberless times I have met the unknown. Often my memory fails me in the anxiety of the moment. In preparation for a new adventure, I often look for *common ground* between this experience and ones of the past, so that I can bolster my courage. Sometimes I remind myself of my successes. And at other times I simply remind myself to trust the process, for memory reminds me that even in the darkness I will find light. Thus both you and I can use our survivorship and our successes to **remember** we are blessed with **courage** and free to try new ways of being in the world.

With time I have developed a **trust** in my ability to meet the unknown. For a long time I thought the issue was trust in others, but have come to realize it's really about my being able to trust my own instincts as well as my ability to cope with disappointments and disloyalties. Back then there were encounters that did not end well. I allowed rejections, abandonments, and failures to suck the very life from me. Long I sat in despair and pity. Yet in the darkness of those times, I found nuggets of light that shone the way to new paths, new knowing, new strengths, and renewed courage. I have come to **trust** my innate drive to grow and learn.

This leads me to another essence—**flexibility**. This seems too common a word to name a quality so necessary for resiliency. Oftentimes we prefer to live in a world of opposites: black or white, yes or no, right or wrong, love or hate, mine or yours, or win or lose. It is an art to live in the world of grays—white gray, gray gray, and black gray. Whenever I paint myself into a white world, I have also created a black world and am stuck in my fear, filled with judgment and arrogance. Does this really serve me or others? I must remind myself that it is seldom a question of "either or" but "both," for all growth requires the death of something so that something new can be born. This is but one of the gifts of the natural world. In today's world of media hype, information overload, and an "us versus them" attitude, it is a constant challenge to be **flexible** enough to find *common ground*

This requires the willingness and ability to **listen and speak from the heart**. The stories herein reflect the essence of my being. The stories have also had a profound impact on how I see, hear, and respond in the world. Each of us has his/her own personal story or narrative; however, to be present to another's story, I must step back from my own story so as to create space for me to be curious about how another's way of being is influenced by his/her story. In holding my story without abandoning or minimizing it, I am **listening** for the *Common Ground* between the other and myself. This frees me to **speak** from my heart using "I" to reflect my thoughts, feelings, and knowing rather than relying on "you"—which leads to judgment, blame, defensive responses, and conflict. When one is received and responded to from the heart, one knows s/he is being held in sacred space.

I recall a time in my early 30's when I was recounting to my dad my climb of Long's Peak using ropes and carabiners for protection from vertical exposure on the East Face. I was giddy with the accomplishment for I was so fearful of heights and the constant danger of falling. My words were simply inadequate to communicate all I was feeling. Finally my dad said he could not really understand what I was talking about, but "it sounds like the same feeling I had when I flew solo for the first time!" No other words were necessary—two heart-starved beings met. What more can one need but to be **heard and acknowledged from the heart?**

What have I learned about groups and their structures?

Each of us has many early and formative experiences in groups—family, play groups, classrooms, and teams. Generally speaking the model of organization in these groups is vertical hierarchy with someone— parent, teacher, coach—in charge. This "power over" model also is reflected in the general organizational structure of businesses, corporate conglomerates, and governments. Principally a male model of organization, the distinct advantages are the expediency of top-down decision-making and control or protection, depending on one's perspective. There are also disadvantages. In hierarchical organization, vision, creativity, and problem solving are in the hands of those in power. How much is missed in not honoring and listening to everyone in a family, community, or organization? And how do we teach our children, teens, and adults to be **responsible for** one's choices and **responsible to** the group without listening and encouraging them to be full participants? With no shared responsibility commensurate with developmental age, one can fall into powerlessness, disinterest, lack of investment, distrust, and despair.

There is another organizational paradigm—"power with." This model is horizontal in structure reflecting a more feminine approach emphasizing connection with others. Here there is inclusion, shared responsibility, and shared decision making based on dialog. This model, too, has its disadvantages. In "power with" the process of decision making is as important as the decision itself, thus the entire process can be time-consuming, slower, and frustrating when time is of the essence or when some become impatient with the process. In this model, everyone is challenged to "show up" and to leave judgments and ego at the door. It requires efforts in listening, clarifying, and working through to consensus. Yet these are skills we all need to develop if we are to grow into responsible beings—**responsible for** ourselves and **responsible to** others.

Neither of these models alone provides an adequate answer for group functioning, cohesion, and growth. Organizationally, the **flexibility** to hold both models without judgment and to know when each may be best is important. How else will we learn how to speak, to listen, to envision, and to act responsibly without family, classroom, and team experiences to be "part of" so that we may carry our gifted selves into our larger communities? Then, too, we must learn when it is necessary for some few or one to speak for the many whether in a family, classroom, or team. A fire is not the time for processing! Thus being **flexible** in a family, classroom, or team is knowing in one's heart when to use which model or a combination.

Throughout this book **circles** have been omnipresent— the Medicine Wheel, the circle of life, the passage of twenty-four hours or a year, or a single experience through the Four Shields. And with repeated trips around the Medicine Wheel, the circle morphs into a spiral, several endlessly connected circles. The **circle** holds all. The **circle** is the foundation for building community whether in a family, classroom, team, neighborhood, or beyond. Many cultures continue to use the **circle** in organization, decision making, and celebrations. **Circles** create equality, presence, process, and dialog. The first time of sitting in a circle I was struck by my vulnerability. Here I was looking eye to eye and being seen eye to eye. With no hiding place, I was transformed from bystander to participant and witness. There are big circles, small circles, and circles within circles. My experience is if you are looking to grow, join a **circle** and, if you want to help others to grow, create a **circle**.

Whether in a family, classroom, neighborhood, or work place, each of us, young and old alike, experiences the stresses of everyday living. When we come together in a circle to discuss, process, decide, or act, it is easy to treat a meeting as just another daily stress and not bring our full attention to the meeting. Thus it is helpful to set the meeting apart from the everyday and to honor it as **sacred time**, for this is when we want to bring our full being forward. **Sacred space** can be created in many different ways—lighting a candle, calling in the four directions, checking-in with one another, striking a bell, singing a song, or offering a prayer are some examples. Likewise, the close of the meeting can be honored in a way that marks a return to the everyday.

Remember all those excuses I would use to avoid risking the unknown? They reflected my experiences of learning it was not safe to be who I was/am. Each of us has experienced the pain of shame and humiliation when who we are is not accepted. Thus an atmosphere of welcoming and openness is essential if group members are to be safe. This can be accomplished in several ways. One way to establish **safety** is to agree to some basic *ground rules* which govern each meeting. It is most helpful if these evolve from the group. A clear statement about the *purpose* of the circle and a working *agenda* focuses the meeting and limits extraneous matters from intruding. Both the purpose and the agenda can be leader-driven, but it is beneficial to have input from all members whenever possible. A general *format* for how the circle will function needs to be established. For example, how will conversation begin and proceed? Will it begin in one place and proceed in orderly fashion around the circle? Will it, instead, occur in random fashion and, if so, how will the next speaker be acknowledged? I have participated in circles in which a "talking stick" or other object is claimed by the person wishing to speak. Must everyone speak or will there be a procedure for "passing"? How shall the circle arrive at decisions?

Confidentiality is an important *ground rule* in creating **safety**. This includes the manner in which each person's feelings and ideas will be treated with respect, both in the circle and beyond. In families it is all too easy to tease about one's vulnerabilities and ideas. This occurs in the classroom, in friendships, on the playing field, in town meeting, and in corporate boardrooms as well. Why would anyone want to be honest, creative, or actively present if s/he is going to become the object of jokes, put-downs, or bullying? And what would it say about me if I were the one doing it or joining in with my laughter? Growing respect for oneself and others is learned in the laboratory of family, friendships, classroom, team, and civic meetings. *Ground rules* should also include the procedures by which reconciliation will occur if a basic rule has been broken. In other words, how will a safe environment be re-established if confidentiality is broken or if disrespect occurs?

These thoughts reflect some of my more positive experiences of sitting in a circle with others. In the bibliography I have listed a few resources which offer much more extensive information.

What must I/you do to live on this planet not as a visitor but as a steward of all that is here?

We live in an increasingly complex, interdependent, fast-paced, and often frightening world. There are times when I am simply overwhelmed by the depth of our disregard for others on this planet. There are times I want to retreat, avoid news reports, and create a cocoon of safety in my little world in the woods of New Hampshire. How silly! Sooner or later, reality sets in. Something often draws me in—my politically-involved neighbors, an incidence of bigotry in a nearby city, a natural cataclysm, the human struggle for freedom, an environment endangered—and I am reminded that there is no escape. I am part of the circle. You are part of the circle. So what do I/you do?

I want to live with an impeccable **attention** to how I am choosing to live my life as a member of a family, a community, a nation, and the planet. I need to be asking myself, "How do I choose to use or conserve our precious resources? How do I contribute to or get in the way of peace and harmony? Do I claim my voice not only on behalf of myself but for others, too, or do I turn away?"

The stories of the Four Shields and the endless travel around the Medicine Wheel illustrate that life is a process. My goal is to continue to grow in my humanity until I leave this physical body and then something else will happen. There is no perfection but there is the journey of always becoming. It is serious play and so I am reminded that **persistence** is necessary. There are always more questions than answers. There are always new adventures in meeting the unknown. We live in uncertain times but are we not lucky to be here in this time to learn from the wisdom keepers who came before us, to use science and technology, to reaffirm our decency, and find our *Common Ground* so that the circle of life can endure?

There are many paths. The Four Shields of the Medicine Wheel is but one. My intention is that the stories, reflections and practices of *Common Ground, Uncommon Gifts* be a guide for seekers and doers as we come together in family, community, national, and international circles to listen deeply, speak from the heart, and honor our diversity, while strengthening the strands of the web that connect us all.

Go forth on your journey,
for the benefit of many,
for the joy of the many,
out of compassion for the welfare,
the benefit and joy of all beings.

The Buddha

Selected Bibliography

DEEP ECOLOGY

Berry, Thomas. *Evening Thoughts: Reflecting on Earth as Sacred Community.* San Francisco: Sierra Club Books, 2006. 171 pp.

Buzzell, Linda and Craig Chalquist, eds. *Ecotherapy: Healing with Nature in Mind.* San Francisco: Sierra Club Books, 2009. 311 pp.

Clinebell, Howard. *Ecotherapy: Healing Ourselves, Healing the Earth.* New York: The Haworth Press, 1996. 293 pp.

Foster, Steven and Meredith Little. *The Four Shields: The Initiatory Seasons of Human Nature.* Big Pine: Lost Borders Press, 1998. 354 pp.

Macy, Joanna and Molly Young Brown. *Coming Back to Life: Practices to Reconnect Our Lives, Our World.* Gabriola Island: New Society Publishers, 1998. 233 pp.

McKibben, Bill. *The End of Nature.* New York: Random House, Inc., 2006. 195 pp.

Plotkin, Bill. *Soulcraft: Crossing into the Mysteries of Nature and Psyche.* Novato: New World Library, 2003. 368 pp.

Sessions, George, ed. *Deep Ecology for the 21ˢᵗ Century: Readings on the Philosophy and Practice of the New Environmentalism.* Boston: Shambala Publication, Inc., 1995. 488 pp.

NATURE AND SPIRIT

Andrews, Ted. *Animal-Speak: The Spiritual and Magical Powers of Creatures Great and Small.* St. Paul: Llewellyn Publications, 1998. 383 pp.

Andrews, Ted. *Nature-Speak: Signs, Omens and Messages in Nature.* Jackson: Dragonhawk Publishing, 2004. 447. pp.

Farmer, Steven D. *Animal Spirit Guides: An Easy-to-Use Handbook for Identifying and Understanding Your Power Animals and Animal Spirit Helpers.* Carlsbad: Hay House, Inc., 2006. 455 pp.

Ingerman, Sandra. *Medicine for the Earth: How to Transform Personal and Environmental Toxins.* New York: Three Rivers Press, 2000. 291 pp.

Johnson, Cait. *Earth, Water, Fire and Air: Essential Ways of Connecting to Spirit.* Woodstock: SkyLight Paths Publishing, 2003. 201 pp.

Luttichau, Chris. *Animal Spirit Guides: Discover Your Power Animal and the Shamanic Path.* New York: CICO Books, 2009. 160 pp.

MacGregor, Catriona. *Partnering with Nature: The Wild Path to Connecting with the Earth*. New York: Atria Paperback, 2010. 289 pp.

May, Gerald. *The Wisdom of Wilderness: Experiencing the Healing Power of Nature*. New York: HarperCollins Publishers, 2006. 194 pp.

Palmer, Jessica Dawn. *Animal Wisdom: The Definitive Guidebook to the Myth, Folklore and Medicine Power of Animals*. London: Thorsons, 2001. 396 pp.

Paterson, Jacqueline Memory. *Tree Wisdom: The Definitive Guidebook to the Myth, Folklore and Healing Power of Trees*. London: HarperCollins Publishers, 1996.

Starhawk. *The Earth Path: Grounding Your Spirit in the Rhythms of Nature*. New York: HarperCollins Publishers, 2004. 245 pp.

CHILDREN AND NATURE

Caduto, Michael and Joseph Bruchac. *Keepers of the Earth. Native American Stories and Environmental Activities for Children*. Golden: Fulcrum, Inc, 1997. 209 pp.

Caduto, Michael and Joseph Bruchac. *Keepers of the Night: Native American Stories and Nocturnal Activities for Children*. Golden: Fulcrum, Inc, 1994. 146 pp.

Llewellyn, Bridget McGovern. *One Child, One Planet*. Auburn Hills: Emerald Shamrock Press, 2009.

Louv, Richard. *Last Child in the Woods: Saving Our Children from Nature-Deficit Disorder.* Chapel Hill: Algonquin Books of Chapel Hill, 2005. 334 pp.

SAVING THE PLANET/SAVING OURSELVES

Baker, Carolyn. *Sacred Demise: Walking the Spiritual Path of Industrial Civilization Collapse.* New York: iUniverse, Inc., 2009. 334 pp.

Bolen, Jean Shinoda. *The Millionth Circle: How to Change Ourselves and the World.* Berkley: Conari Press, 1999. 87 pp.

Brown, Lester R. *Plan B 4.0: Mobilizing to Save Civilization.* New York: W. W. Norton & Company, 2009. 368 pp.

Carnes, Robin Deen and Sally Craig. *Sacred Circles: A Guide to Creating Your Own Women's Spirituality Group.* New York: HarperCollins Publishers, 1998. 215 pp.

Ehrenfeld, John R. *Sustainability by Design: A Subversive Strategy for Transforming Our Consumer Culture.* New Haven: Yale University Press, 2008. 246 pp.

Gilley, Kay. *Leading From the Heart: Choosing Courage over Fear in the Workplace.* Boston: Butterworth-Heinemann, 1997. 267 pp.

Horowitz, Claudia. *The Spiritual Activist: Practices to Transform Your Life, Your Work and Your World.* New York: Penguin Putnam Inc., 2002. 257 pp.

Mindell, Arnold. *The Deep Democracy of Open Forums: Steps to Conflict Prevention and Resolution for the Family, Workplace and World.* Charlottesville: Hampton Roads Publishing Company, Inc., 2002. 201 pp.

Zimmerman, Jack and Virginia Coyle. *The Way of Council.* Las Vegas: Bramble Books, 1996. 308 pp.

About the Author

BARBARA A. MEYERS, MSW

Like the ever-widening circles created when a stone is dropped into still water, the natural world has enveloped Barbara's life. From her first experience of a small wriggling fish at the end of a homemade pole and line, she has been captured by the wonders of nature. That wonder and curiosity have been steady companions all the years of her life. Visiting farms and later growing up on a farm provided lots of opportunities for exploring woods and streams and all the wildlife therein. As a young adult she undertook to learn the skills and knowledge for being in the wilderness. She has camped, hiked, solo backpacked, rock climbed, canoed, snow- and ice-climbed, snowshoed and cross-country skied throughout the Northeast and in the mountains and canyons of the West.

Her vocations have been two—teacher and clinical social worker/therapist. After earning a Master's Degree from Smith College, she taught general college students and both undergraduate and graduate students pursuing careers in physical education and recreation. Later her teaching career expanded to include outdoor education and led to organizing and leading wilderness experiences for teens and adults with an emphasis on living with nature, not against it.

In mid-life, she left formal teaching to return to school to earn a Master's Degree in Social Work from the Northern New England Branch of the University of Connecticut School of Social Work. Today as a private practitioner she works with families, adults, teens, and children in individual and group settings. She also organizes and leads groups for clients and workshops for clinicians. As a therapist and workshop leader, she continues to draw upon stories and lessons from the natural world in guiding others along their paths to peace and harmony. In 2006 she was honored to receive recognition as New Hampshire's Social Worker of the Year.

She is drawn to earth-based experiences as a means for continuing her own journey. In recent years she has studied at The School of Lost Borders in Big Pine, California. The School, founded by Stephen Foster and Meredith Little, trains individuals from around the world in the essential aspects of modern cross-cultural rites of passage. In workshops including Ceremonies of the Night, Coyote, Mirroring, and Vision Quest, Barbara was introduced to the Medicine Wheel. Her journey continues with shamanic wisdom-keeper Sandra Corcoran, founder of Starwalker Adventures.

Her focus continues to be on deepening her own experiences and understanding of earth-based traditions of the Americas so that she may share that with others.

She can be reached at PO Box 528, Henniker, NH 03242 or via email at journey@mcttelecom.com.